Atlas
OF ANIMALS

American edition published in 2013 by Millbrook Press, a division of Lerner Publishing Group, Inc.

First published in 2012 by Weldon Owen Limited
Northburgh House, 10 Northburgh Street
London EC1V 0AT, UK

Millbrook Press
A division of Lerner Publishing Group, Inc.
241 First Avenue North
Minneapolis, MN 55401 U.S.A.

Website address: www.lernerbooks.com

Main body text set in TheSans Kind ExtraLight 13/18.

Library of Congress Cataloging-in-Publication Data

Johnson, Jinny, 1949–
    Animal Planet atlas of animals / by Jinny
Johnson.
      pages   cm
    Includes index.
    ISBN 978–1–4677–1327–6 (lib. bdg. : alk. paper)
    ISBN 978–1–4677–1691–8 (eBook)
    1. Zoogeography—Juvenile literature. I. Animal
Planet (Television network) II. Title. III. Title:
Atlas of animals.
    QL101.J64 2012
    591.4'2—dc23   2013001746

Manufactured in the United States of America

1 — BP — 7/15/13

Atlas
OF ANIMALS

Jinny Johnson

Contents

North America   18

Africa   60

Asia   76

Central and South America

Europe

Australasia

Poles and Oceans

The Animal Kingdom

THERE ARE TWO MAIN GROUPS of animals. The invertebrates—animals without backbones—include creatures such as insects and spiders. Scientists think there may be millions more invertebrates yet to be discovered. Mammals, birds, reptiles, amphibians, and fish are vertebrates—animals with backbones. The approximate number of species is given for each type of animal.

Insects
There are more insects than any other kind of creature. Most are small and have six legs, two pairs of wings, and a pair of antennae on their head.

305,250

Other invertebrates
Land-based invertebrates include spiders, worms, and snails. In the sea, there are many more, such as crabs, sponges, clams, and jellyfish.

Bony fish

31,300

Fish
There are two kinds of fish. The bony, or ray-finned, fish are the largest group. They have skeletons made of bone. Cartilaginous fish, such as sharks and rays, have skeletons made of a gristly material called cartilage.

Cartilaginous fish

Birds
A bird has two legs, a pair of wings, and a body covered with feathers. Birds are the only animals that have feathers.

9,998

1,000,000

Invertebrates 95%

Vertebrates 5%

Number of species About 95 percent of the 1.3 million or so known animal species are invertebrates. Vertebrates make up only 5 percent of total numbers.

5,490

Mammals
Mammals come in many shapes and sizes, but all are warm-blooded and have a bony skeleton. Most have a covering of hair and well-developed senses.

6,433

Amphibians
There are three groups of amphibians—salamanders and newts, frogs and toads, and wormlike caecilians. Amphibians were the first land vertebrates.

9,084

Reptiles
Turtles, snakes, lizards, and crocodiles are all reptiles. Most have a covering of tough, waterproof scales.

Evolution and Adaptation

Trilobite

NATURE DOESN'T STAND STILL. Animals and plants are constantly changing and adapting to their surroundings. Sometimes these changes create new species, while other species die out. The process of change is called evolution. We know something about how life on Earth has evolved over millions of years from fossils. Fossils are the remains of animals and plants that have gradually turned to rock.

200 million years ago

90 million years ago

Changing world
The movements of Earth's surface plates have caused great changes in the shapes of our landmasses. The continents are still on the move today.

Today

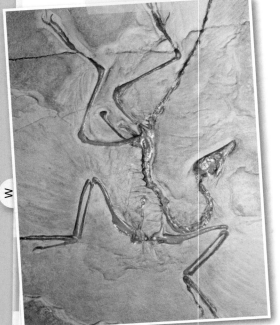

The history of life on Earth
Most scientists agree that Earth was formed about 4.5 billion years ago. This diagram shows when different forms of life are thought to have evolved.

Key
- ☐ Archean era
- ☐ Proterozoic era
- ☐ Paleozoic era
- ☐ Mesozoic era
- ☐ Cenozoic era
- ▬ Mass extinction
- *bya* billion years ago
- *mya* million years ago

Evidence from the past
The fossilized skeleton above is of *Archaeopteryx*, which lived in the days of the dinosaurs. It is generally believed to be the earliest-known bird.

Fossil of an ammonite, an extinct mollusk

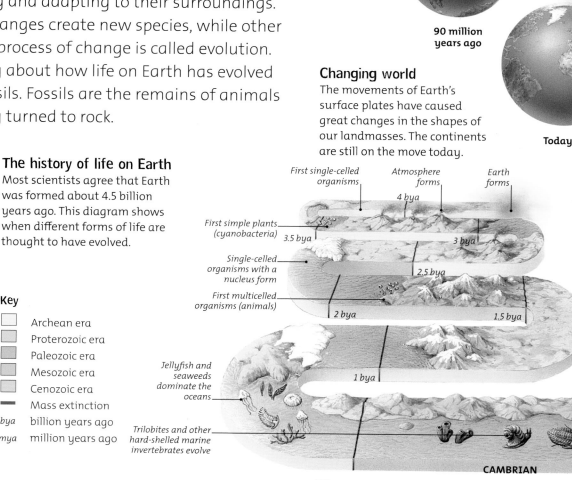

First single-celled organisms

Atmosphere forms

Earth forms

4 bya

First simple plants (cyanobacteria) 3.5 bya

3 bya

Single-celled organisms with a nucleus form

2.5 bya

First multicelled organisms (animals)

2 bya

1.5 bya

Jellyfish and seaweeds dominate the oceans

1 bya

Trilobites and other hard-shelled marine invertebrates evolve

CAMBRIAN

550 mya

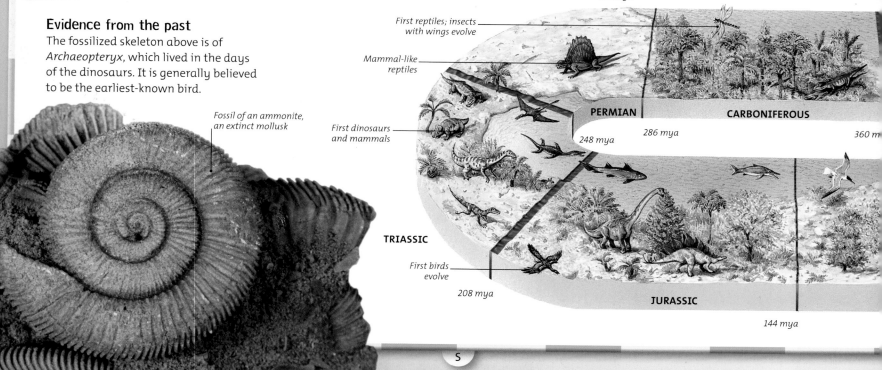

First reptiles; insects with wings evolve

Mammal-like reptiles

First dinosaurs and mammals

PERMIAN

CARBONIFEROUS

248 mya

286 mya

360 m

TRIASSIC

First birds evolve

208 mya

JURASSIC

144 mya

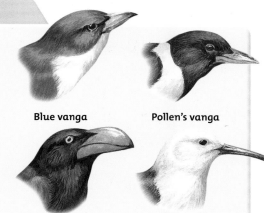

Big beak and
featherless
head

Broad wings
with deep slots
for gliding

**African
vulture**

Strong feet and
sharp talons

American turkey vulture

Shaped for scavenging

Two kinds of birds, African vultures and New World
vultures such as the turkey vulture, have evolved a
similar appearance. They share the same scavenging
habits—feeding on dead animals.

▶▶▶ FIT FOR LIFE

NATURAL SELECTION On the
island of Madagascar, a single
species of vanga has evolved
into 14 different species. These
resemble birds from different
groups that do not occur on
the island. The vangas have
developed dramatically
different beak shapes to suit
the kind of food they eat.

Blue vanga

Pollen's vanga

Helmet vanga

Sickle-billed vanga

Shark (fish)

Evolution in action

A sleek, torpedo-shaped body and
strong back fins help an animal move
fast through water. Sharks, dolphins, and
the extinct ichthyosaurs all belong to
different animal groups but have evolved
similar shapes for swimming speed.

Tapering body
shape

**Ichthyosaurus
(reptile) fossil**

Dolphin (mammal)

Human impact

Humans evolved less than
two million years ago—a
blink of the eye in terms of
the history of our planet.
But our species has had a
greater impact on Earth
than any other.

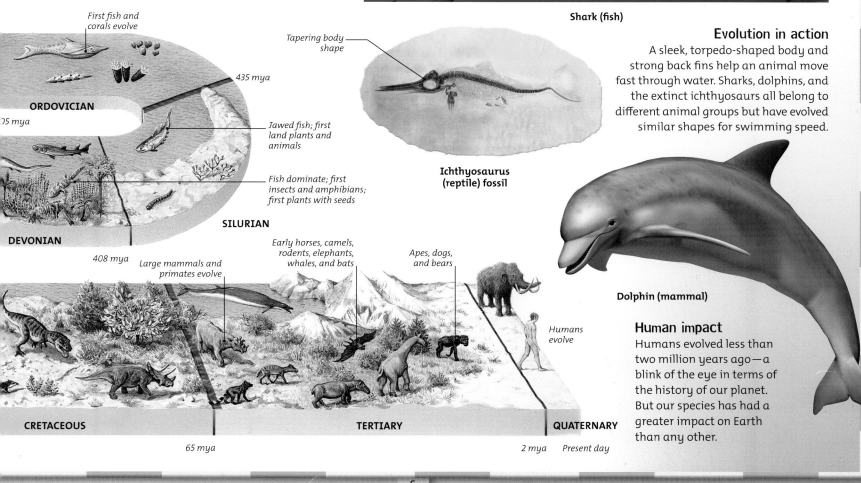

First fish and
corals evolve

435 mya

ORDOVICIAN

5 mya

Jawed fish; first
land plants and
animals

DEVONIAN

Fish dominate; first
insects and amphibians;
first plants with seeds

SILURIAN

408 mya

Large mammals and
primates evolve

Early horses, camels,
rodents, elephants,
whales, and bats

Apes, dogs,
and bears

Humans
evolve

CRETACEOUS

TERTIARY

QUATERNARY

65 mya

2 mya   Present day

Eating to Survive

FINDING ENOUGH FOOD is a constant struggle for animals. Nearly everything, other than top predators, is food for something. But the higher a creature is in the food chain, the fewer individuals of that species there will be. The whole interacting system is based on the energy output from the sun being trapped by green plants.

Who eats whom?

In this example of a food chain in a North American field, grasshoppers feed on the plants, and mice and other small creatures gobble up the insects. At the top of the food chain is a predatory hawk.

Hawk

Mice

Grasshoppers

Green plants

Top predators

Few other animals can catch top predators, such as eagles. The short-toed eagle catches snakes and other animals, which in turn feed on smaller animals, such as mice.

▶▶▶ FIT FOR LIFE

SEED EATER The crossed tips of a crossbill's beak make a perfect tool for taking seeds from pinecones. The bird inserts its beak into the cone, forcing the scales apart so it can reach the seed. Different species have larger or smaller beaks to suit the types of cones they feed on.

Red crossbill on a pinecone

From shrimps to shark

Shrimps eat plants and other tiny food items in the sea. Fish snap up the shrimps and are food for the ocean's top predators, such as sharks.

Wasp larvae in silken cocoons

Living on others

A parasite makes its home on its food supply. Some wasps lay their eggs inside caterpillars. When the young hatch, they eat their way out of the caterpillar.

Scavengers

Little is wasted in the natural world. Scavengers, such as hyenas and vultures, are always ready to eat up animals that die naturally and to steal any leftovers from lions and other hunters.

IN FOCUS

SEARCHING FOR GRASS Some animals have to make long journeys called migrations to make sure they have food all year round. Rain falls at different times of the year in the various parts of the Serengeti. Wildebeests follow the rains to get the best grazing.

Lake Victoria

KENYA

August–October

TANZANIA

June–July

November–May

Migratory paths

Serengeti National Park

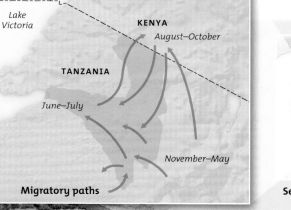

The Living World

NATURE DIVIDES THE WORLD not into countries and continents but into natural regions, according to how hot or cold the climate is and how much rainfall there is. This determines what kind of plant life grows— for example, whether it is forest or grassland. Animals depend on plants, so the type of plant life affects which animals can live in each region and how they adapt to conditions. Desert animals, for instance, must be able to survive with little water. Creatures in boreal forests have to live through severe winters.

Lemur

Boreal forests
These forests of coniferous trees grow across northern North America and Eurasia. Summers are hot, and winters are extremely cold.

Vegetation zones
The map here shows the world's main natural regions, but large areas of some of these have been dramatically changed and disrupted by human activities.

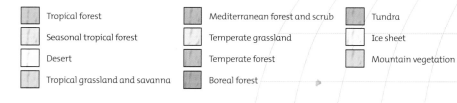

- Tropical forest
- Seasonal tropical forest
- Desert
- Tropical grassland and savanna
- Mediterranean forest and scrub
- Temperate grassland
- Temperate forest
- Boreal forest
- Tundra
- Ice sheet
- Mountain vegetation

NORTH AMERICA

SOUTH AMERICA

▶▶▶ FIT FOR LIFE

ENDEMIC ANIMALS Some animals and plants are spread across wide areas and different habitats. Others are endemic to one area—that is, they are found nowhere else. An animal can be endemic to a particular region, such as the Gobi Desert, or to a much smaller area, such as an island or lake.

The kagu is found only on the island of New Caledonia in the South Pacific Ocean. This flightless bird is now rare.

The Baikal seal lives only in Lake Baikal in Siberia. Baikal is the world's oldest lake.

Tropical rainforest
It is always hot and always wet in these forests, and they contain an extraordinary range of plant and animal life.

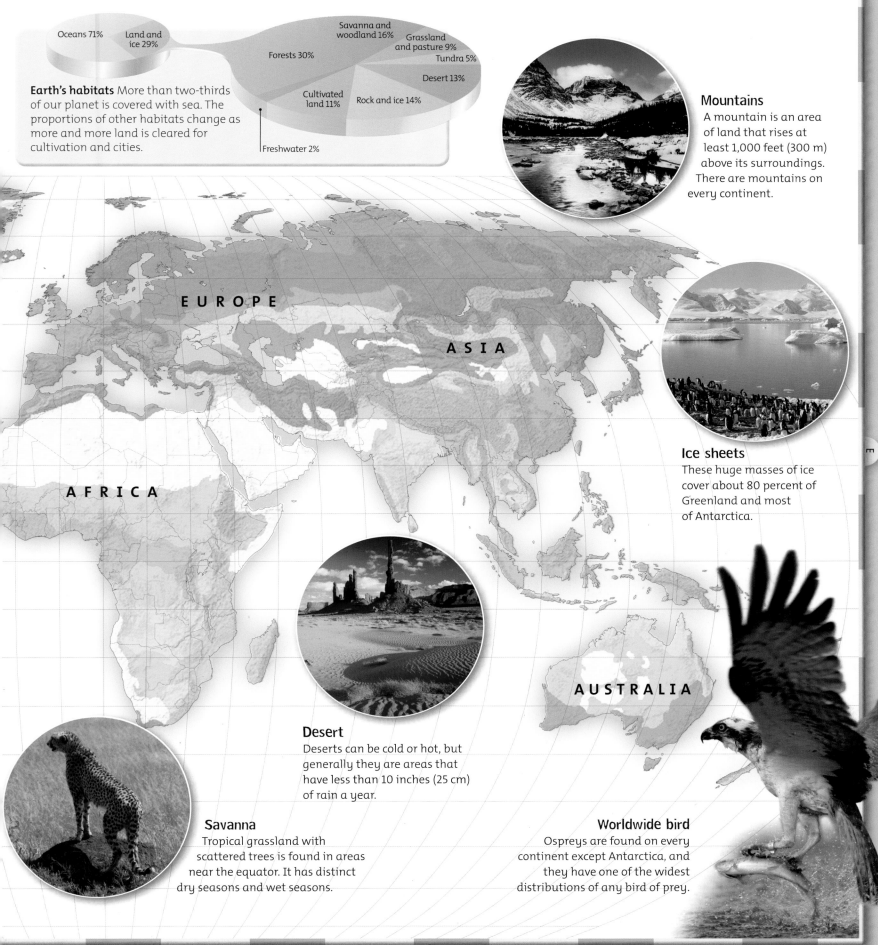

Oceans 71%   Land and ice 29%

Savanna and woodland 16%

Grassland and pasture 9%

Forests 30%

Tundra 5%

Desert 13%

Earth's habitats More than two-thirds of our planet is covered with sea. The proportions of other habitats change as more and more land is cleared for cultivation and cities.

Cultivated land 11%   Rock and ice 14%

Freshwater 2%

EUROPE

ASIA

AFRICA

AUSTRALIA

Mountains
A mountain is an area of land that rises at least 1,000 feet (300 m) above its surroundings. There are mountains on every continent.

Ice sheets
These huge masses of ice cover about 80 percent of Greenland and most of Antarctica.

Desert
Deserts can be cold or hot, but generally they are areas that have less than 10 inches (25 cm) of rain a year.

Savanna
Tropical grassland with scattered trees is found in areas near the equator. It has distinct dry seasons and wet seasons.

Worldwide bird
Ospreys are found on every continent except Antarctica, and they have one of the widest distributions of any bird of prey.

Animals and People

HUMANS have always used other animals in various ways. We have long hunted and eaten them, we use their fur and other body parts, and we have tamed and domesticated them to keep on farms and as pets. Many animals work for us—elephants, camels, and donkeys carry heavy loads; dogs are trained to help the blind and disabled, and to work with the police and rescue services. But other creatures are not as welcome because they spread disease or destroy our food crops.

Mosquito

City hunter
Hawks and falcons are adaptable birds, and many are taking to city life. They swoop down on prey from skyscrapers instead of from mountain crags.

Red queleas

Urban scavenger
Animals such as foxes and raccoons have learned to make the most of city life, scavenging on the food that we throw away.

City birds
Pigeons are common in cities all over the world. They used to nest and perch on cliffs, but now they use buildings and rooftops.

Crop destroyers
Flocks of thousands, even millions, of queleas swoop down and destroy whole fields of grain crops in minutes.

Spreading disease
Brown rats have spread all over the world and are one of the most serious pests. They spoil huge quantities of stored food, kill other animals, and spread disease.

Cattle ranch
Humans have kept cattle and other animals for at least 8,000 years to provide us with meat, milk, and skins.

Working animals
Sled dogs are still used as a means of transportation in some parts of the far north, and racing with sled dogs has also become a popular sport.

▶▶▶ FIT FOR LIFE

WILD ANCESTORS By selective breeding over thousands of years, humans have domesticated animals and reared them to have the characteristics we can best use for food and for work.

The red jungle fowl lives in southern and Southeast Asia and is said to be the ancestor of our domestic hens.

Przewalski's horse is the only truly wild horse left in the world and may be one of the ancestors of domestic horses.

Swarm of locusts
Locusts are a kind of grasshopper. They gather in huge swarms and can inflict devastating damage to plants. The largest-known swarm contained as many as 40 billion insects.

Animals in Danger

TIGERS AND ORANGUTANS are just two of the many animals in danger of becoming extinct—disappearing from the world forever. While some extinctions have always been a natural part of life, the rate is much, much higher now than it has ever been, and this is due to human activities. Conservation efforts are vital if we are to save at least some of these creatures.

Trade in animals
Countless wild animals are illegally caught and sold as pets, as well as for their horns, shells, and skins. This is the second most serious threat to wildlife after habitat destruction.

Shrinking habitat
Orangutan numbers are dangerously low, mostly because so much of their rainforest home has been cleared to grow palm oil and other crops.

◀◀ STRUGGLING FOR LIFE

ON THE RED LIST The Bornean orangutan and the animals shown below are all critically endangered. This means that there are so few of them left in the wild that they could soon become extinct. Information like this is gathered by an organization called the International Union for the Conservation of Nature (IUCN). They keep a "Red List" of endangered species.

Orange-bellied parrot

Corroboree frog

Baiji

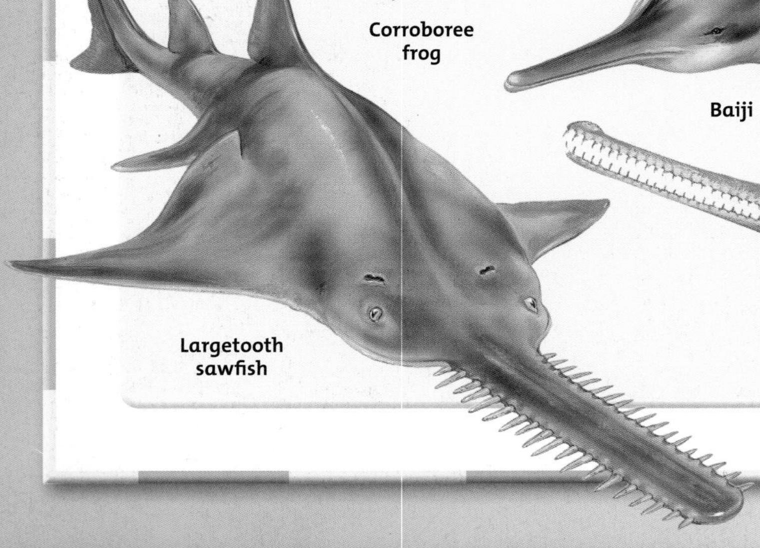

Largetooth sawfish

Gharial

Urban wetlands
A wetland reserve, close to the center of London, England, has proved to be a successful haven for wildlife. The reserve is home to more than 180 kinds of birds, as well as small mammals, bats, and insects.

Nature reserves
The world's growing population puts more and more pressure on land, and habitat loss is the greatest single threat to animal life. Nature reserves and national parks ensure the survival of at least some areas of unspoiled land, where animals and plants can live undisturbed.

◉ IN FOCUS

SAVING THE CALIFORNIA CONDOR Thirty years ago there were only about 25 of these magnificent birds left in the wild. Thanks to successful conservation measures, the condor has survived and there are now 191 birds living in the wild.

Condor chicks that have been hatched and reared in captivity are now being released into the wild to boost numbers.

North America

A HUGELY VARIED LAND, North America features snowcapped mountain ranges, vast deserts, and grassy plains, as well as towering forests. Some natural regions, such as the prairie, have been greatly reduced by farming and industry, but there is still much to enjoy, and the many national parks are world famous. Wildlife highlights include bison, pronghorn, bears, and alligators.

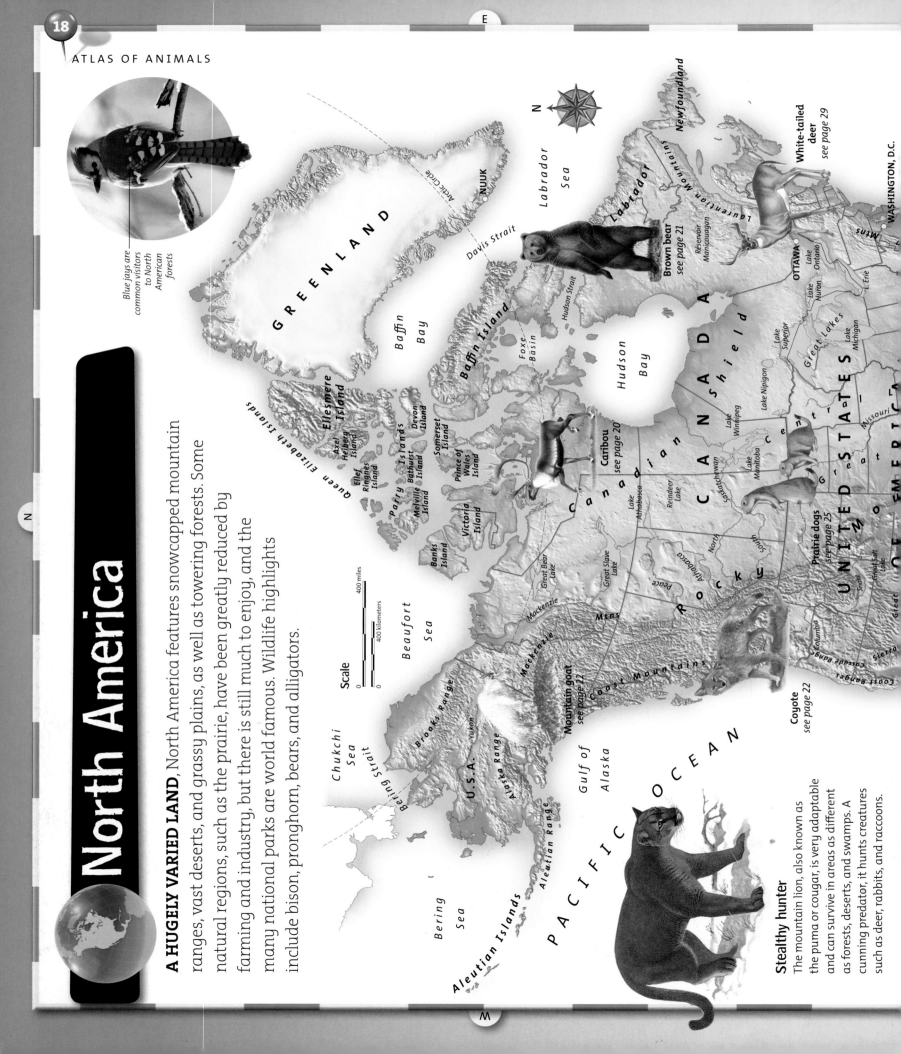

Blue jays are common visitors to North American forests

Stealthy hunter

The mountain lion, also known as the puma or cougar, is very adaptable and can survive in areas as different as forests, deserts, and swamps. A cunning predator, it hunts creatures such as deer, rabbits, and raccoons.

N

E

N

W

Scale

400 miles

400 kilometers

0

0

White-tailed deer
see page 29

Brown bear
see page 21

Caribou
see page 20

Prairie dogs
see page 25

Mountain goat
see page 22

Coyote
see page 22

GREENLAND

Arctic Circle

NUUK

Labrador Sea

Newfoundland

Laurentian Mountains

Réservoir Manicouagan

Labrador

Davis Strait

Baffin Bay

Baffin Island

Hudson Strait

Foxe Basin

Hudson Bay

OTTAWA

Lake Superior

Lake Huron

L. Ontario

L. Erie

Lake Michigan

Great Lakes

Ellesmere Island

Axel Heiberg Island

Ellef Ringnes Island

Queen Elizabeth Islands

Parry Islands

Bathurst Island

Melville Island

Devon Island

Somerset Island

Prince of Wales Island

Victoria Island

Banks Island

CANADA

Canadian Shield

Lake Nipigon

Lake Winnipeg

Lake Manitoba

Saskatchewan

Reindeer Lake

Lake Athabasca

Great Slave Lake

Great Bear Lake

North Saskatchewan

South Saskatchewan

Athabasca

Peace

Mackenzie

Mackenzie

UNITED STATES OF AMERICA

Great Plains

Central

Missouri

WASHINGTON, D.C.

Mtns

Rocky Mtns

Coast Mountains

Cascade Range

Sierra

Coast Ranges

Columbia

Snake

Great Salt Lake

Beaufort Sea

Chukchi Sea

Brooks Range

Alaska Range

Aleutian Range

U.S.A.

Yukon

Gulf of Alaska

Bering Strait

Bering Sea

Aleutian Islands

PACIFIC OCEAN

ATLANTIC OCE

see page 31

Tropic of Cancer

Mississippi Delta

Coastal Plain

Gulf of Mexico

Yucatan Peninsula

see page 26

Gulf-Atlantic

Rio Grande

MEXICO

Sierra Madre Oriental

Sierra Madre Occidental

MEXICO CITY

Sierra Madre del Sur

Sierra Madre

Sonoran Desert

Gulf of California

Baja California

Record breaker

The pronghorn is the fastest-running animal in North America. It races across the prairie at more than 53 miles per hour (86 km/h) and can keep going for many miles at this speed.

IN FOCUS

MIGHTY EAGLE The bald eagle, a symbol of the United States, is a magnificent bird of prey. At one time, though, hunting and damage by pesticides reduced its numbers so much that it was in danger of extinction. Now it is strictly protected, and bird numbers are on the rise. Bald eagles make one of the biggest of all birds' nests. A nest can be as much as 9½ feet (3 m) wide.

Bald eagle's nest

The mighty bison

Bison are the heaviest land animals in North America. They were nearly wiped out during the 19th century. Now smaller herds roam the plains again, feeding on grasses and shrubs.

NATURAL REGIONS

Northern Forests ◯ see pages 20–21

Great Plains ◯ see pages 24–25

Eastern Forests ◯ see pages 28–29

Rocky Mountains ◯ see pages 22–23

Western Deserts ◯ see pages 26–27

Coastal Plains ◯ see pages 30–31

Northern Forests

Canada goose

VAST AREAS of spruce, fir, and other coniferous trees grow across northern North America. Although the winters are long, cold, and snowy, a variety of mammals, such as bears, wolverines, and flying squirrels, make their home here. In the summer, many more birds fly into the forests to feast on the abundant insect life. The stretch of forest along the Pacific Northwest is one of the richest on Earth and contains magnificent evergreens, such as the redwoods, which are among the tallest and longest-living of all trees.

N

Beaufort Sea

Anchorage

Gulf of Alaska

Whitehorse

Yellowknife

Juneau

Great Slave lake
Fort Smith

Hudson Bay

La

Goo

Edmonton

Lake Winnipeg

Vancouver

Regina

Winnipeg

Québec

Seattle

OTTAWA

Portland

Helena

Toronto

Bos

Boise

New York

Chicago

WASHING

St. Louis

Atlanta

P A C I F I C   O C E A N

Forest lakes

There are many lakes, ponds, and other wetlands in these northern forests. They are home to a range of waterbirds, including ducks, cranes, kingfishers, and loons.

American porcupine

A porcupine may have as many as 30,000 sharp quills, which makes it a difficult animal for a predator to attack. Porcupines are good climbers and feed on bark, leaves, fruits, and buds.

Powerful hunter

The fierce wolverine is the largest member of the weasel family. It hunts rabbits and rodents and also attacks much larger animals, including caribou, but it eats forest berries in the summer.

Caribou on the move

Caribou, also known as reindeer, spend the winter in the south of this region. In the summer, they trek north to fresh feeding grounds.

W

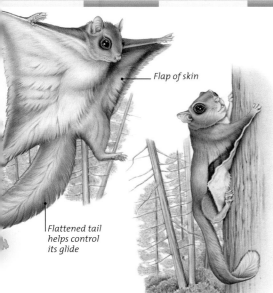

▶▶▶ FIT FOR LIFE

SURVIVING THE SNOW Some animals, such as the Canada lynx and the snowshoe hare, have specially adapted furry feet to help them survive in their snowy home. These act like "snowshoes" to keep them warm and stop them from sinking into the snow.

Canada lynx

Snowshoe hare

In the summer, the snowshoe hare has brown fur. In the winter, its coat turns white to blend in with the snow and help it hide from predators, such as the lynx.

Flap of skin

Flattened tail helps control its glide

Flying squirrel

This squirrel doesn't really fly, but it does glide from tree to tree. As it leaps into the air, it spreads the flaps of skin at the sides of its body, and these act like a parachute to help the squirrel glide gently through the air.

Big bear

Bears are the biggest carnivores in North America, but for much of the year they feed mostly on nuts, berries, and leaves. In the summer, when salmon are swimming upriver to breed, the bears plunge into the water to feast on the fish.

IN DANGER! The whooping crane is officially endangered, but numbers are now on the rise, thanks to conservation work. Birds bred in captivity have also been released into the wild. This is the tallest bird in North America.

Rocky Mountains

Rattlesnake

THE PEAKS of the Rocky Mountains carve a dramatic path across western North America. They extend from northern Canada to New Mexico, a distance of at least 3,000 miles (4,830 km). The highest points of the Rockies reach 14,400 feet (4,390 m). Winters are cold here, but summers are generally mild, and most areas have plentiful rain. Some of the most spectacular animals on this continent, such as bison, gray wolves, and mountain lions, make the Rockies their home.

Sure-footed climbers

Mountain goats are perfectly at home among mountain crags. Their specially adapted hooves help them grip and balance, and their long, thick fur keeps them warm in the biting winter winds.

IN FOCUS

PACK ANIMALS Gray wolves live in packs led by a dominant male and female pair. Most packs contain around 8 to 10 animals, but there may be 20 or more where there is plenty of prey. Wolves hunt in a pack, working together to ambush and kill large animals, such as deer and moose.

Wolf cubs

Coyote

Smaller than a wolf and with a bushier tail, the coyote is more common in the southern Rockies, where there are fewer wolves. Coyotes eat rabbits, rodents, and even insects.

Beaufort Sea

Anchorage

Whitehorse   Yellowknife

Gulf of Alaska

Juneau

Hudson Bay

Jasper

Vancouver   Regina   Winnipeg   Québec

Seattle   OTTAWA

Portland   Helena   Toronto

Boise   New York

Salt Lake City   Chicago   WASHINGTON

San Francisco   Denver   St. Louis

Kansas City

Los Angeles   Memphis   Atlanta

San Diego   Phoenix   Dallas

El Paso   Austin   Miami

NUU

La

PACIFIC OCEAN

Rocky Mountains

▶▶ FIT FOR LIFE

EXPERT BUILDER The American beaver makes more changes to its surroundings than any creature other than humans. It cuts down trees to dam streams, creating huge ponds, and builds lodges for shelter and food supplies.

Beavers have webbed feet for swimming power and large paddle-shaped tails that act like rudders. Their teeth and jaws are extremely strong.

The lodge is made of branches, leaves, and mud

Winter food supplies are also kept underwater

Entrances to the lodge are underwater

IN DANGER! The western toad is still common in the northern Rockies but is becoming rare farther south. It spends much of its time underground in burrows and catches worms, insects, and other small creatures.

Learning to hunt
Mountain lions generally live and hunt alone, except for mothers and cubs. From about six months old, cubs go hunting with their mother to learn her skills.

Mountain bluebird
This beautiful bird is common throughout the Rockies. Insects are its main food, although it also eats seeds and berries. It nests in tree holes.

Bighorn sheep
Agile bighorn sheep climb high in the Rockies to escape from wolves and coyotes. Only the males have big curving horns, which they use in fierce battles over females.

Great Plains

Grasshopper

AT THE HEART of North America, the Great Plains cover around 1,000 miles (1,600 km) between the Rocky Mountains and the Missouri River. Also known as the prairie, this was once a huge area of grassland, grazed by herds of animals such as bison and pronghorn antelope. Now much of it is used for agriculture and cattle ranching, but some prairie does remain. The climate is generally dry, with scorching-hot summers and cold, snowy winters. Many small mammals, birds, and insects make their home here.

N

PACIFIC

Edmonton

Vancouver · Regina · Winnipeg

Seattle

Portland · Helena

Boise · Cheyenne · Ch

Salt Lake City · St. L

San Francisco · Denver

Kansas City

Los Angeles · Memp

San Diego · Phoenix · Dallas

El Paso · Austin

OCEAN

Rocky Mountains

Great Plains

Prairie grasses

The many kinds of grasses that grow on the Great Plains provide plentiful food for pronghorn and other animals. In the drier western prairie, grasses are shorter than in the wetter east.

Plains spadefoot toad

This toad burrows into sandy soil, using the spadelike structure on each of its back feet. When it rains, the toad emerges to mate and lay eggs.

Burly bison

The huge bison, with its heavy shoulders and shaggy fur, is at least 6½ feet (2 m) tall at the shoulder and weighs a ton (910 kg). Males and females live in separate herds but come together in the summer for the mating season.

Summer visitors
Swainson's hawks spend the summer months in the Great Plains area, preying on mammals, birds, and other creatures. In the winter, they migrate more than 6,000 miles (10,000 km) to South America.

IN DANGER! Once common throughout the Great Plains, the black-footed ferret nearly became extinct in the 20th century. It is now protected, and captive-bred animals have been released into the wild.

Great horned owl
This owl nests on trees, buildings, and cliffs. The owl lays one to four eggs, and she and her mate feed their owlets small prey such as rabbits, squirrels, and birds for at least six weeks.

Prairie songbird
The western meadowlark is common on the prairie, where it gathers grain and weed seeds with its slender beak and snaps up insects.

Strong digger
Strong and stocky, the American badger is an expert digger and makes itself an underground den, where it spends most of the winter months.

IN FOCUS

BUSY BURROWERS Prairie dogs are rodents, like rats and mice. These little animals live in colonies and dig burrows with many rooms and tunnels. Within the burrows there are areas for sleeping, looking after young, and even toilets. The prairie dogs work together to find food, protect the nest, and look out for danger. They feed on grass, roots, and seeds.

Grass is an important food.

Long-eared leaper
The black-tailed jackrabbit is actually a hare, not a rabbit. It is a fast runner and can make great leaps on its long back legs.

AWA

New York

GTON, D.C.

tlanta

Western Deserts

Grasshopper mouse

THERE ARE TWO KINDS of deserts in this area. To the south are the hot deserts: the Mojave, Sonoran, and Chihuahuan, with their searing summer temperatures and low rainfall. Each has its characteristic plant life, such as Joshua trees in the Mojave and mesquite scrub in the Chihuahuan, as well as a range of animals that have managed to adapt to and survive in desert conditions. To the north of these hot deserts is the Great Basin—a cold desert. The sagebrush plant grows on this high, dry scrubland.

Desert snake

The sidewinder snake travels across the soft sand with a sideways movement, pushing against the ground with two parts of its body. As it moves, it leaves a trail of parallel markings in the sand.

Saguaro cactus

Dominating the landscape of the Sonoran Desert is the saguaro cactus. These cacti grow slowly but can reach a height of 50 feet (15 m) after 100 years or more.

Battling tortoises

Desert tortoises feed on tough desert grasses in the morning and evening and spend the rest of the day in shady burrows. Males have fierce battles when they meet, each trying to turn over the other.

Nectar feeder

The little Costa's hummingbird hovers by desert flowers, feeding on nectar. It also eats tiny insects and spiders.

▶▶ FIT FOR LIFE

KEEPING COOL Many desert predators stay hidden during the heat of the day and come out to hunt at dusk, when temperatures are falling. A snake's thick, scaly skin also helps reduce water loss from the body.

Diamondback rattlesnake

The deadly scorpion kills its prey by injecting venom with the stinger at the end of its tail.

N

Portland

Boise

Salt Lake City

San Francisco

Great Basin

Denver

Los Angeles

Mojave Desert

San Diego

Sonoran Desert

Phoenix

Tucson

El Paso

Da

Chihuahuan Desert

Chihuahuan

Monterrey

PACIFIC OCEAN

Gulf of California

W

S

Chicago
WASHINGTON, D.C.
St. Louis

Memphis   Atlanta

New
Orleans

Gulf of
Mexico

Chuckwalla

This plant-eating lizard has a very clever way of protecting itself. If attacked, it wedges itself into a little crack in a rock, then puffs up its body so it is almost impossible to get out.

The barrel cactus is common in the Sonoran Desert

Extra-long lower shell used in battles

Kangaroo rat

The tiny desert kangaroo rat can live without drinking any water. It gets all it needs from the seeds and other plant food that it eats.

IN FOCUS

WATER IN THE DESERT When rain does fall, the saguaro cactus can store huge amounts of water in its fleshy pulp for use in drier times. The cactus is home to birds, such as the gila woodpecker and the elf owl, which nest in its branches and catch insects that live on the plant.

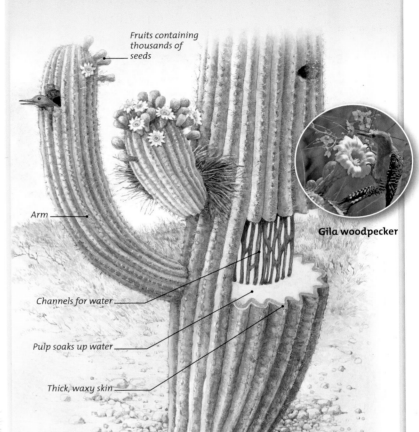

Fruits containing thousands of seeds

Gila woodpecker

Arm

Channels for water

Pulp soaks up water

Thick, waxy skin

Trunk

Black widow spider

This spider does have a very venomous bite, but it uses it to kill insect prey. It only bites humans in self-defense.

IN DANGER! At 2 feet (60 cm) long, the gila monster is a large lizard. It is also one of the few venomous lizards in the world. The gila is becoming increasingly rare, due to the destruction of its natural habitat and trapping by collectors.

Eastern Forests

Raccoon

OAKS, MAPLES, BEECH, and other deciduous trees dominate these forests. They once covered the entire eastern side of North America, but large areas have been destroyed to build cities and create farmland. The forests that remain contain a wide variety of smaller trees, shrubs, ferns, and fungi, as well as the splendid trees. They are rich in wildlife too, with a particularly wide variety of birds and amphibians. The area enjoys long, warm summers, and the spring and fall are usually mild, but winters can be harsh. There is normally plenty of rain all year round, so plant life flourishes.

Forests in the fall
In the fall, these deciduous trees turn to rich hues of yellow, gold, and red, as their leaves die and fall. Some birds fly south for the winter, but the northern cardinal remains in the forests all year round.

Wild turkey
These large birds can fly but find most of their food on the forest floor. Acorns are a favorite item, but the turkey also eats grasses, seeds, and insects.

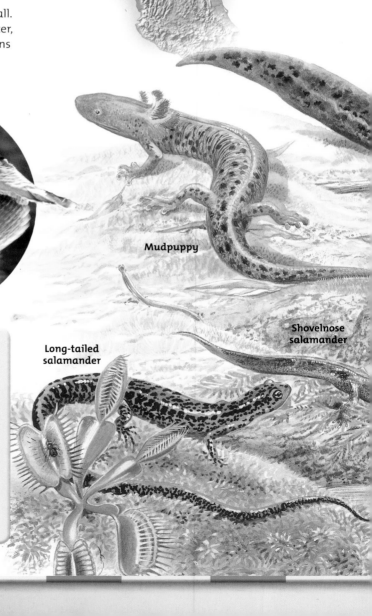

Mudpuppy

Shovelnose salamander

Long-tailed salamander

IN FOCUS

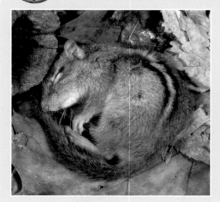

HIBERNATION Winters can be bitterly cold in this area, and hibernation can help animals survive. Chipmunks and others retreat to a warm burrow for the winter months. The body temperature falls, and the heartbeat slows so the animal uses as little energy as possible.

Chipmunk in hibernation

N

W

S

Edmonton

Vancouver
Seattle
Portland

Regina
Winnipeg

Helena
Boise

Salt Lake City

San Francisco
Denver

Los Angeles
San Diego
Phoenix
El Paso

OTTAWA
Toronto
Ne

WASHINGT

Lake
Michigan
Chicago
Indianapolis
St. Louis

Kansas
City

Memphis
Atlanta

Dallas

Austin
New
Orleans

Monterrey

*Gulf of
Mexico*

Appalachian Mt

▶▶▶ FIT FOR LIFE

HELPING EACH OTHER Oak trees are common in these forests, and their acorns are food for many kinds of animals, including deer, mice, and chipmunks. The chipmunks also prey on gypsy moths. This helps the oak trees, as gypsy moth caterpillars can gobble up huge amounts of their leaves.

Black-legged tick

White-tailed deer

Acorn

Chipmunk

Gypsy moth

White-footed mouse

When acorns are plentiful, deer thrive but so do the ticks that live on them. Ticks can also bite humans and spread Lyme disease.

Virginia opossum
An expert climber, this marsupial spends much of its life in trees. It feeds on anything it can find, including nuts, small animals, garbage, and carrion.

Forest salamanders
There are more salamanders in these forests than anywhere else on Earth. They live in and around streams and hide in damp spots under logs and rocks. Most feed on insects, worms, and other small creatures.

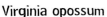

Eastern hellbender

Jordan's salamander

Black-bellied salamander

Pygmy salamander

Smelly skunk
If attacked, the striped skunk lifts its tail and sprays a smelly, oily liquid made by glands near its tail. This puts off most predators, who then stay away from skunks in the future.

Winter sleep
Also known as the woodchuck, the groundhog depends on plentiful supplies of leaves, berries, and grasses in the summer. It then retires to its burrow and hibernates during the winter.

Speedy hunter
Around the snout of the star-nosed mole are 22 highly sensitive tentacles. The mole uses these to sniff out prey on land and in water with astonishing speed.

Coastal Plains

Pond slider turtle

THE SWAMPS of Louisiana, the Florida Everglades, and the long, sandy beaches of the Atlantic coast are all features of this relatively flat region of the United States. Although much of this area is now heavily populated and land is used for farming and industry, there is still plenty of wildlife in the natural regions that remain. Alligators and many kinds of turtles and fish live in the swamps, and huge flocks of birds stop off on these coasts on their journeys to and from wintering grounds.

Small prey is swallowed whole

Skin is heavily armored

Marshland birds
Reedbeds in freshwater marshes are home to birds, such as the black-crowned night heron, which nest and shelter here among the reeds.

Cottonmouth snake
This large snake spends much of its life in water and is fairly common in swamps, rivers, and wetlands in this area. It kills fish, frogs, and birds with its venomous bite.

Top predator
The American alligator can catch and kill more or less anything in its powerful, toothy jaws. It lies in wait in the water, only its eyes and nose visible, ready to rear out to catch prey.

▶▶▶ FIT FOR LIFE

WILDLIFE HABITAT Large areas of bamboo, known as canebrakes, once grew along streams and creeks in this area, but only scattered patches now remain. Many kinds of birds and small mammals shelter here to hide from predators, and the caterpillars of butterflies and moths feed on cane leaves.

Giant bullfrog

Indigo bunting

Northern cardinal

Swainson's warbler

Creole pearly-eye

Golden mouse

Swamp rabbit

Yehl skipper

Louisiana waterthrush

Snail eater

Snails are the main food of the Everglade kite, and its beak is perfectly shaped for this diet. The bird holds the shell in its talons, then inserts its beak to twist out the flesh.

Sea cow

The gentle manatee, also known as the sea cow, lives in coastal waters and enters estuaries and rivers in Florida. It feeds on water plants, including sea grasses and algae.

Elegant egret

This beautiful member of the heron family lives around salt marshes and ponds as well as along coasts. It feeds on small shrimps and fish, which it seizes in its long, slender beak.

Armored armadillo

The body of the nine-banded armadillo is protected by bands of heavy horn, making it very hard to attack. It roots around on the ground for insects and also swims well.

Central and South America

THE WORLD'S LARGEST RIVER and highest lake are among the wonders of South America. The fourth-largest continent, it contains widely contrasting landscapes, such as lush tropical rainforest, vast rolling grasslands, and the towering Andes Mountains. Central America is the narrow bridge of land that links North and South America. Like South America, it is home to an astonishing range of wildlife.

IN FOCUS

GALAPAGOS ISLANDS These islands are in the Pacific Ocean, off the coast of Ecuador, and some very unusual reptiles, found nowhere else in the world, live there. These include giant tortoises—the world's largest—and the marine iguana, the only sea-living lizard.

Marine iguana

Giant tortoise

Squeezing to death

The boa constrictor, like its larger cousin the anaconda, doesn't kill prey by venom but by squeezing its victim until it suffocates.

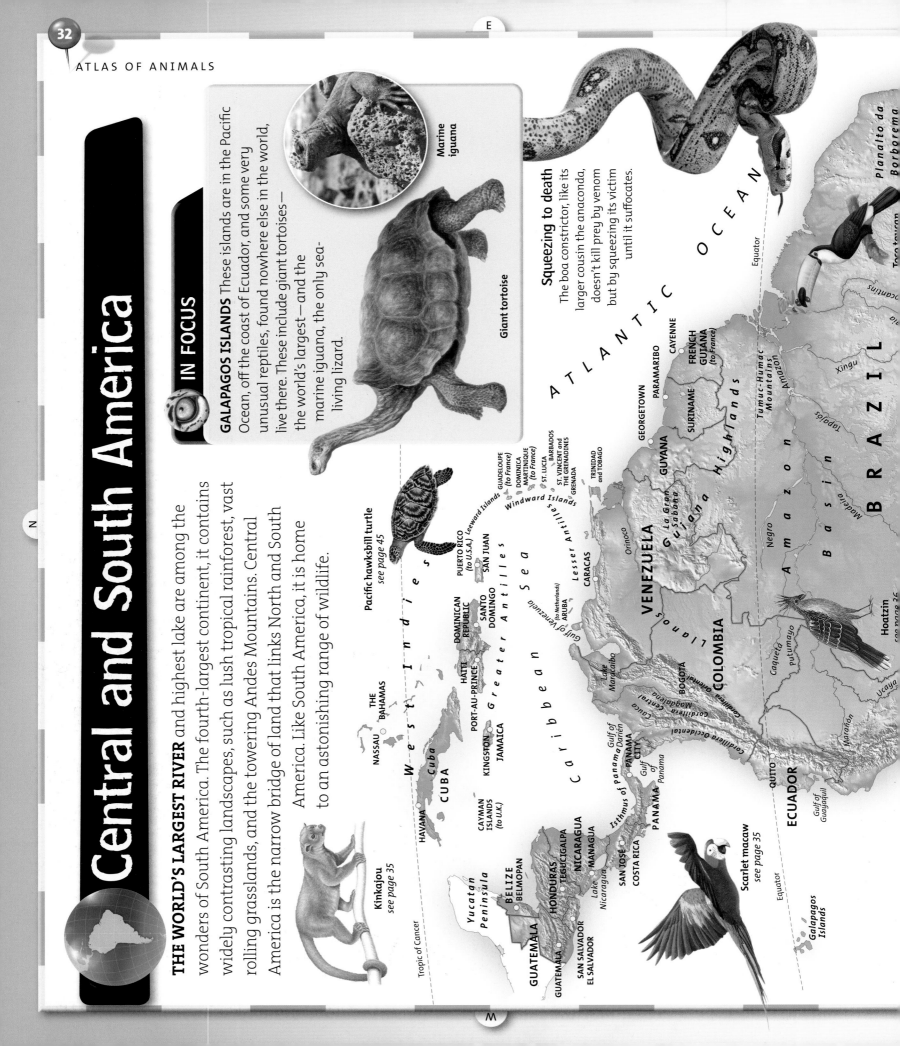

Kinkajou
see page 35

Pacific hawksbill turtle
see page 45

Scarlet macaw
see page 35

Hoatzin
see page 26

ATLANTIC OCEAN

Equator

Equator

Tropic of Cancer

THE BAHAMAS
NASSAU

CUBA
HAVANA

CAYMAN ISLANDS
(to U.K.)

HAITI
PORT-AU-PRINCE

DOMINICAN REPUBLIC
SANTO DOMINGO

JAMAICA
KINGSTON

PUERTO RICO
(to U.S.A.)
SAN JUAN

West Indies

Greater Antilles

Leeward Islands

GUADELOUPE (to France)
DOMINICA
MARTINIQUE (to France)
ST. LUCIA
BARBADOS
ST. VINCENT and THE GRENADINES
GRENADA

Windward Islands

Lesser Antilles

TRINIDAD and TOBAGO

Caribbean Sea

Yucatán Peninsula

GUATEMALA
GUATEMALA

BELIZE
BELMOPAN

HONDURAS
TEGUCIGALPA

EL SALVADOR
SAN SALVADOR

NICARAGUA
MANAGUA

Lake Nicaragua

COSTA RICA
SAN JOSE

PANAMA
PANAMA CITY

Gulf of Panama

Isthmus of Panama

Gulf of Darién

Gulf of Venezuela
(to Netherlands)
ARUBA

CARACAS

VENEZUELA

Lake Maracaibo

Orinoco

La Gran Sabana

Guiana Highlands

GEORGETOWN
GUYANA

PARAMARIBO
SURINAME

CAYENNE
FRENCH GUIANA
(to France)

Tumuc-Humac Mountains

Planalto da Borborema

BRAZIL

Amazon Basin

Amazon

Negro

Xingu

Tapajós

Madeira

COLOMBIA
BOGOTÁ

Magdalena

Cauca

Cordillera Occidental

Cordillera Central

Cordillera Oriental

Caquetá

Putumayo

ECUADOR
QUITO

Gulf of Guayaquil

Galapagos Islands

Llanos

Marañón

Ucayali

South

N

E

W

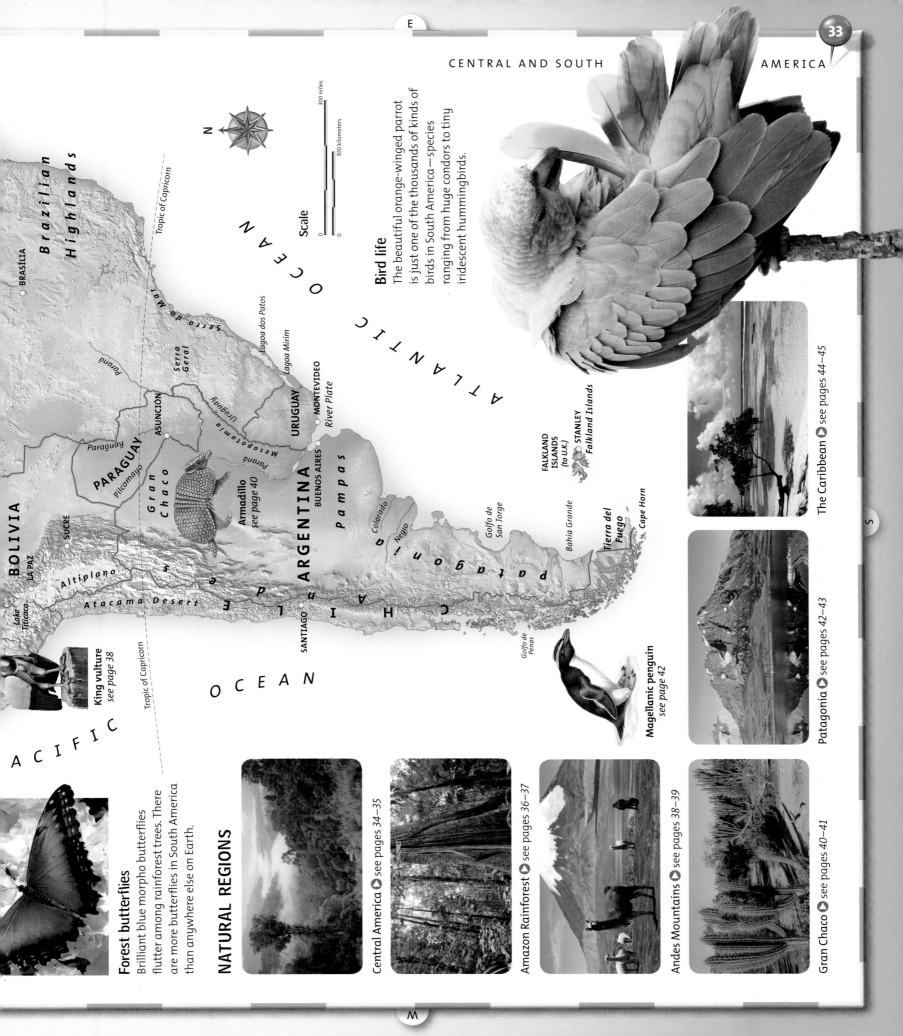

Bird life

The beautiful orange-winged parrot is just one of the thousands of kinds of birds in South America—species ranging from huge condors to tiny iridescent hummingbirds.

Scale

300 miles

300 kilometers

N

ATLANTIC OCEAN

PACIFIC OCEAN

Brazilian Highlands

BRASÍLIA

Serra do Mar

Serra Geral

Lagoa dos Patos

Lagoa Mirim

Paraná

Paraguay

BOLIVIA

LA PAZ

SUCRE

Lake Titicaca

Altiplano

Atacama Desert

PARAGUAY

ASUNCIÓN

Pilcomayo

Gran Chaco

Mesopotamia

Uruguay

Paraná

URUGUAY

MONTEVIDEO

River Plate

BUENOS AIRES

ARGENTINA

Pampas

Colorado

Negro

Golfo de San Jorge

Bahía Grande

Patagonia

Golfo de Penas

Tierra del Fuego

Cape Horn

FALKLAND ISLANDS (to U.K.)

STANLEY

Falkland Islands

CHILE

SANTIAGO

Andes

Tropic of Capricorn

Armadillo
see page 40

King vulture
see page 38

Magellanic penguin
see page 42

Forest butterflies

Brilliant blue morpho butterflies flutter among rainforest trees. There are more butterflies in South America than anywhere else on Earth.

NATURAL REGIONS

Central America ▶ see pages 34–35

Amazon Rainforest ▶ see pages 36–37

Andes Mountains ▶ see pages 38–39

Gran Chaco ▶ see pages 40–41

Patagonia ▶ see pages 42–43

The Caribbean ▶ see pages 44–45

N

Central America

Blue morpho butterfly

DENSE TROPICAL RAINFOREST used to cover nearly all of Central America, but much has now been cleared to make way for towns and farmland. In the areas of rainforest that remain, there are countless species of insects, as well as snakes, frogs, monkeys, and colorful birds. All flourish in this jungle land, where the weather is hot and wet all year long.

Nesting quetzal

Quetzal
In the mating season, the beautiful male quetzal grows two amazing tail feathers up to 2 feet (0.7 m) long. When he has found a mate, they make a nest in a tree hole.

Yucatan Peninsula

BELMOPAN

Golfo de Honduras

Caribbean Sea

GUATEMALA

TEGUCIGALPA

Cabo Gracias á Dios

SAN SALVADOR

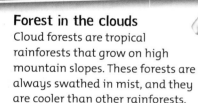

Forest in the clouds
Cloud forests are tropical rainforests that grow on high mountain slopes. These forests are always swathed in mist, and they are cooler than other rainforests.

W

MANAGUA

Lake Nicaragua

Tree frogs
Tiny tree frogs spend nearly all their lives high up in the forest. They can climb tree trunks with the help of their special feet, which have sticky pads under each toe. These help the frog hold on tight.

PACIFIC OCEAN

SAN JOSÉ

Golfo de los Mosquitos

PANAMA CITY (PANAMÁ)

Gulf of Panama

IN FOCUS

COOL TOUCANS Scientists used to think a toucan had a long beak so it could reach fruits at the end of branches. Now they believe that a toucan's big beak helps it stay cool. The toucan seems to be able to increase blood flow to the beak in order to lose heat and cool down.

Jungle cat
The largest big cat in Central and South America, the jaguar is one of the biggest of all jungle hunters. Deer, peccaries, and tapirs are its main prey, but it also catches fish and turtles.

Keel-billed toucan

Toco toucan

Channel-billed toucan

S

Woolly
monkeys

Harpy
eagle

Sloth

Kinkajou

Howler
monkey

Spider
monkeys

*The kinkajou's tail
is about the same
length as its body*

Scarlet
macaw

Toucan

Life in the canopy

The rainforest canopy, made up of the crowns of trees, is
where most jungle animals live, and many of these seldom
go down to the ground. One of the main predators that these
treetop dwellers have to watch out for is the ferocious harpy
eagle, which hunts monkeys and sloths. Birds, such as toucans
and macaws, feed on fruits and nuts growing on the trees.

Noisy monkey

The male howler monkey
has the loudest voice of any
monkey, and its bellowing
screams can be heard up to
3 miles (5 km) away. The call
warns other monkeys to stay
far away.

*The poison-dart
frog puts each
tadpole in a
separate pool*

Gripping tail

The agile kinkajou has a
prehensile (gripping) tail that it
uses to hold on to and hang
from branches as it climbs
among the forest trees. The tail
also helps the kinkajou balance.

*Tightly packed
leaves form a
water-holding tank*

Treetop pools

For tree dwellers, such as poison-dart
frogs, water can be a long way down.
So they put their tadpoles in the pool
of water at the center of a bromeliad,
where they can develop in safety.

Amazon Rainforest

Spider monkeys

THE WORLD'S LARGEST tropical forest, the Amazon jungle extends over a huge area of northern South America, covering parts of nine countries. Always hot and always wet, it is the richest natural area on Earth. An amazing variety of animals live in the forest—almost a third of all the species on Earth. Experts believe there are many more kinds of plants and animals that have yet to be discovered.

The mighty Amazon
Experts disagree about whether the Amazon or the Nile is the longest river, but the Amazon carries more water. It is 4,000 miles (6,400 km) long and flows through the Amazon rainforest to the Atlantic.

River dolphin
The Amazon dolphin is one of the few freshwater dolphins. Sensitive hairs on its beaklike snout help it find prey in the muddy river water.

Hoatzin have a crest of spiky red feathers

Hoatzin
The hoatzin is one of the few birds that feeds almost entirely on leaves. Its digestive system is adapted to cope with this diet.

Strong body coils squeeze prey until it suffocates

Jaws can open wide to swallow big prey

Safety measure
The pattern on a young tapir's coat helps it hide from predators in the dappled light of the forest floor. The tapir loses its spots and stripes when it is a year old.

Anaconda
One of the fiercest hunters in the Amazon River is the anaconda—the world's largest, heaviest snake. It swallows even large prey whole, and one big meal can last for months.

IN FOCUS

HARPY EAGLE One of the biggest and most powerful of all eagles, the harpy has huge talons, measuring up to 5 inches (13 cm), for killing its prey. It flies with great skill among the forest trees chasing prey, such as monkeys and sloths, which it grasps in its strong feet.

Layers of the forest

A tropical rainforest can be divided into different layers, each with its own plant and animal life. The canopy and understory are home to the greatest number of animals, including many monkeys and birds. The forest floor is the quietest area.

Algae grows on the sloth's fur, giving it a greenish tinge

Three-toed sloth

Sloths spend nearly all their time in the trees, hanging on to branches with their long claws. On the ground, they can only drag themselves along.

Camouflaged hunter

The ocelot is a superb jungle hunter. Its markings help it hide among the leaves, and it climbs and even swims well.

Black caiman

The caiman is a type of crocodile that lives in the Amazon, where it preys on fish and mammals such as capybara. It can grow to more than 13 feet (4 m) long.

EMERGENT

Orange-winged amazon

CANOPY

Black spider monkey

Three-toed sloth

Orange-winged amazon

Channel-billed toucan

UNDERSTORY

Green anaconda

FOREST FLOOR

Andes Mountains

Hillstar hummingbird

THE LONGEST MOUNTAIN RANGE in the world, the Andes stretch for about 5,000 miles (8,000 km) down the western side of South America. The landscape is varied, ranging from tropical cloud forests on the lower slopes to desert plateaus and craggy peaks. Some extraordinary animals and plants live here, and 50 percent of them are unique to the area.

N

CARACAS

GEORGETOWN
PARAMARIBO

BOGOTÁ

CAYENNE

QUITO

Equator

A
n
d
e
s

LIMA

Cuzco

Lake
Titicaca

LA PAZ

BRASÍLIA

SUCRE

A
n
d
e
s

ASUNCIÓN

PACIFIC OCEAN

ATLANTIC OCEAN

SANTIAGO

Rugged beauty
The northern part of the Andes is near the equator, so the climate is milder. Farther south, the weather is colder and the landscape rugged and barren.

Furry chinchilla
The chinchilla's thick, soft fur keeps out the cold. Sadly, though, this animal is now rare because so many have been killed for their fur.

King vulture
The king vulture tears into carcasses with its hooked beak, then plunges its head in to feed. The head is bare of feathers.

Giant anteater
This animal is perfectly adapted for eating ants and termites. It uses its strong claws to tear open nests, then gathers up the insects with its long, sticky tongue. It eats up to 30,000 insects a day.

Young anteater rides on mother's back

Long, sticky tongue

Cunning predator
The Andean red fox is also known as the culpeo. It kills poultry and livestock as well as small mammals, so it is unpopular with farmers.

W

S

▶▶▶ FIT FOR LIFE

HIGH LIFE The guanaco and vicuna, and their domesticated relatives llamas and alpacas, are well suited to mountain life. Their thick coats keep them warm, and they have extra-large hearts and lungs to make the most of what oxygen there is.

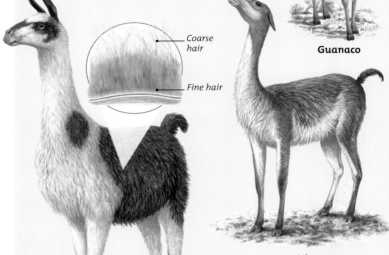

Coarse hair

Fine hair

Guanaco

Vicuna

Llama

A llama has a double coat. There is an under layer of fine, soft hair and an outer coat of long, coarse hair.

Carrion feeder
The Andean condor is one of the largest of all flying birds. It soars for miles over the mountains, searching for carrion (dead animals) to eat.

Display dances
Male cock-of-the-rocks perform a spectacular display dance in the mating season. They build their nests on rocky cliff ledges.

Andean tapir
The tapir is a good climber and also swims well, using its prehensile snout like a built-in snorkel. It feeds on plants.

Pudu
The pudu stands only 15 inches (38 cm) high at the shoulder and is about twice the weight of a domestic cat. It is the world's smallest deer.

IN DANGER! One of the smallest bears, the spectacled bear is now rare and considered vulnerable to extinction. Its face markings are unique—no two bears have exactly the same pattern.

Gran Chaco

Paradox frog

THE LARGE FLAT PLAIN of the Gran Chaco is bordered to the west by the Andes Mountains. It is a wild, remote region, covered with tall grassland and scrubby forest. There are few roads or towns, but lots of animal life—in fact, the name chaco comes from the local Quechua word *chaku*, which means "hunting land." At least 18 kinds of armadillos live here, and it is one of the last places where the rhea is found in any numbers.

Surviving the heat

In the summer, this is one of the hottest areas in South America, and plant life needs to be tough to survive. One common tree is the toborochi, which stores water in its swollen trunk.

Maned wolf

This member of the dog family has unusually long legs. These help it move among, and see over, the tall grasses that grow in this area.

IN FOCUS

HEAVILY ARMORED An armadillo carries its very own body armor in the form of bands of bony plates across its back. These vary in number—the six-banded armadillo (*right*) may have six to eight bands. Armadillos dig open ant and termite nests with their strong claws and feast on the insects.

Only the three-banded armadillo can roll itself up into a ball to defend itself when attacked.

Burrowing owl

This owl can dig its own burrows but often takes over one dug by an armadillo. It hunts on the ground and eats insects and other small creatures, which it catches with its feet.

Map labels: LIMA, Lake Titicaca, LA PAZ, SUCRE, BRASÍLIA, Pilcomayo, Las Lomitas, Bermejo, ASUNCIÓN, Tropic of C, PACIFIC OCEAN, SANTIAGO, Andes, BUENOS AIRES, MONTEVIDEO, ATLANTIC OCEAN

▶▶▶ FIT FOR LIFE

SPEEDY BIRD The rhea is the largest bird in South America. It cannot fly, but it does have long legs and can run at up to 37 miles an hour (60 km/h) to escape from predators. As it runs, it uses its wings to help it balance. Its long legs also help the rhea see over tall grasses.

The rhea has three toes on each of its strong feet. Strong leg muscles help power its fast running.

Night monkey
Also known as the douroucouli, this monkey sleeps during the day and wakes up at night. Its huge eyes help it find food, such as insects and fruits, at night.

IN DANGER! The Chaco peccary is found only in this part of South America and is now endangered, largely due to hunting. The many cacti that grow in the area are its main food, but it also eats roots, fruits, and sometimes catches small mammals.

Torrent duck
The torrent duck lives around fast-flowing streams and is a strong swimmer. It dives into even the most turbulent water and fishes for insects and mollusks.

Unlike most birds, the male tinamou incubates the eggs

Tinamou
The tinamou is a ground-living bird. It can fly but usually prefers to scurry around on the ground. There are a number of species, and all feed on roots, seeds, fruits, and insects.

Patagonia

Magellanic penguins

THIS RUGGED LAND lies at the very tip of South America and includes wide, windswept plains, high mountains, desert, and forest. Winters are bitterly cold and summers very hot, making this a challenging place to live. Most of the area is sparsely populated by humans, but there is abundant wildlife, including foxes, wild cats, and unique rodents. Elephant seals and Magellanic penguins come to the Patagonian shores to breed.

PACIFIC OCEAN

ASUNCIÓN

SANTIAGO

BUENOS AIRES

MONTEVIDEO

Neuquén

ANDES

ATLANTIC OCEAN

Golfo de San Jorge

Falkland Islands

Tierra del Fuego

Cape Horn

N

W

S

Grassy plains

The snowcapped Andes tower over the high, grassy plains that make up part of the Patagonian landscape. Guanaco and other animals come here to graze.

Steamer duck

This duck gets its name from its habit of flapping its wings like a paddle steamer as well as using its feet to push itself through the water.

IN FOCUS

THE BIGGEST SEAL The southern elephant seal is the largest of all the seals—males grow up to 20 feet (6 m) long. Like its namesake, the male has a trunk, which it can inflate to show off to rival males before engaging in fierce battles. Elephant seals spend most of their time in water and are good swimmers and divers. They come to land to mate and give birth.

Female elephant seals are much smaller than males.

Bird thief

The southern caracara is a kind of falcon and a fierce bird of prey. It feeds mostly on the carcasses of dead animals but also steals from other hunters and kills prey for itself.

Geoffroy's cat
This cat adapts easily to many habitats. It climbs well with the help of its sharp claws and hunts small prey, such as birds, lizards, and insects, usually at night.

▶▶ FIT FOR LIFE

UNUSUAL RODENTS The mara might look like a deer, but it is a rodent and belongs to the guinea pig family. Its long legs help it run and jump with ease in this rugged country. Viscachas are much smaller rodents but can run fast among the rocks. All feed on plants.

Plains viscacha

Southern viscacha

Patagonian mara

IN DANGER! Darwin's frog, discovered by Charles Darwin himself, is now rare because of the loss of parts of its forest home. The male frog keeps his tadpoles safe in his vocal sac until they grow into tiny froglets.

Patagonian pumas
Pumas, known as mountain lions in North America, are the largest carnivores in Patagonia. Guanacos are their main prey, but they also hunt rodents, rabbits, and other small creatures.

Patagonian fox
This small fox lives in family groups, and the male brings food while the pups are young. When they are three months old, the young join their parents in the hunt.

The Caribbean

Cuban tody

THE CLEAR WATERS of the Caribbean Sea cover an area of about 1,063,000 square miles (2,754,000 km²). The weather is warm all year long, and the water temperature is an average of 80.6°F (27°C), making this an ideal place for coral reefs. The sea is home to many kinds of corals and other invertebrate creatures and more than 500 species of fish. Wildlife on the islands includes a particularly wide variety of birds, reptiles, and amphibians, although many are now rare.

N

ATLAN

Tropic of Cancer

HAVANA

Yucatan Peninsula

Greater

PORT-AU-PRINCE

Grand Cayman

SA DOM

Antille

Caribbean Sea

PACIFIC

SAN JOSÉ

PANAMA CITY

OCEAN

W

S

Caribbean islands
A chain of more than 7,000 islands, islets, and reefs stretches 2,500 miles (4,000 km) across the Caribbean Sea. At least half of the animal and plant species here are unique to the area.

Butterfly fish
This fish gathers small creatures from crevices in the coral reef with its small protruding jaws. Its eye spot helps confuse predators.

Toothy fish
The teeth of a parrot fish are connected to a strong beaklike structure. The fish uses this to bite off lumps of coral as it feeds.

New coral polyps bud off one another

Coral polyp

Coral reef
An astonishing array of creatures live on coral reefs. The reef itself is made up of the skeletons of millions of coral animals, or polyps, which are relatives of sea anemones.

Queen conch
This large sea-living creature is a mollusk— a type of snail. It grows to about 12 inches (30 cm) long.

Reef octopus

This octopus comes out at night to hunt shellfish and small fish. It sometimes spreads out its eight arms like a tent to form a trap for prey.

Sharp, pointed beak that gives the turtle its name

IN DANGER! Hawksbill turtles are now critically endangered. Like all turtles, they have suffered from the loss of nesting and feeding areas, and they get caught in fishing nets. Hawksbills are also hunted for their shells.

Flippers beat like wings to move the turtle through water

Caribbean reef shark

This sleek, streamlined shark is one of the most common around reefs in this area, and cruises around the coral feeding on smaller fish. It grows to nearly 10 feet (3 m) long.

IN FOCUS

DEADLY BITE One of the few poisonous mammals in the world, the solenodon kills prey, such as insects and spiders, with its venomous bite. There are two species— one in Cuba and the other in Hispaniola.

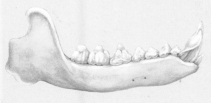

When the solenodon bites, venom flows from a special gland through grooves in its teeth and into the prey.

Crab-eating bird

A common sight on Caribbean shores, the scarlet ibis uses its long, curving beak to probe mud and shallow water for food. Its color comes from the shrimps and other crustaceans that it eats.

Europe

Red fox
This predator is found all over Europe, as well as in Asia and North America. It is now the most widespread wild member of the dog family.

HUGE FORESTS once covered much of Europe, the second smallest of the world's continents. Some forest remains, particularly in the north, but much has been lost to farmland, towns, and cities. Large predators, such as bears and wolves, are now rare, but there are plenty of foxes, weasels, and other smaller carnivores, as well as plant-eating animals such as red deer and wild sheep. There is also a rich range of bird life, from eagles to garden songbirds.

Endangered cat
Ten years ago, only about 100 Iberian lynx remained in the wild. Conservation measures and a captive breeding program have succeeded in raising numbers to about 300.

Octopus
see page 59

Badger
see page 48

Marmot
see page 55

N

W

S

REYKJAVIK
ICELAND

Arctic Circle

Norwegian Sea

Barents Sea

FAROE ISLANDS
(to Denmark)

Inarijärvi

Kjölen Highlands

Lappland

NORWAY

SWEDEN

FINLAND

Scandinavian Shield

Gulf of Bothnia

Lake Ladoga

Shetland Islands

Orkney Islands

Outer Hebrides

British Isles

Atlantic

SCOTLAND

North Sea

OSLO

Skagerrak

STOCKHOLM

Åland

HELSINKI

Gulf of Finland

TALLINN

ESTONIA

Lake Peipus

Vänern

Vättern

Gotland

Öland

Baltic Sea

Gulf of Riga

LATVIA
RĪGA

NORTHERN IRELAND

REPUBLIC OF IRELAND
DUBLIN

ISLE OF MAN
Irish Sea

Pennines

UNITED KINGDOM

Kattegat

Jylland
DENMARK
COPENHAGEN
Fyn

Sjaelland

Bornholm

LITHUANIA
VILNIUS

RUSSIAN FEDERATION

WALES

ENGLAND

Thames

LONDON

NETHERLANDS
THE HAGUE
AMSTERDAM

Badger

BERLIN

WARSAW

North
BELARUS

MINSK

CHANNEL ISLANDS
(to U.K.)

English Channel

BELGIUM
BRUSSELS

Rhine

GERMANY

POLAND

Atlantic Ocean

PARIS

LUXEMBOURG

Harz Mtns

PRAGUE

CZECH REPUBLIC

Carpathian Mountains

UKRAINE

Bay of Biscay

FRANCE

Black Forest

Bohemian Forest

SLOVAKIA
BRATISLAVA

MOLDOVA

Gulf of Gascony

BERN

L.Geneva

SWITZERLAND

LIECHTENSTEIN

VIENNA

AUSTRIA

BUDAPEST

Great Hungarian Plain

ROMANIA

Massif Central

Alps

Dolomites

SLOVENIA

LJUBLJANA

ZAGREB
CROATIA

Pyrenees

ANDORRA

MONACO

SAN MARINO

BOSNIA AND HERZEGOVINA
SARAJEVO

BELGRADE

Transylvanian Alps

BUCHAREST

LISBON

Iberian

MADRID

SERBIA

Danube

PORTUGAL

Peninsula

Sierra Morena

SPAIN

Ligurian Sea

Corsica

Tyrrhenian Sea

VATICAN CITY
ROME

Apennines

ITALY

Adriatic Sea

MONTENEGRO
PODGORICA

PRISTINA
KOSOVO

BULGARIA

SOFIA

Rhodope Mtns

MACEDONIA

Majorca

Minorca

Ibiza

Balearic Islands

Sardinia

TIRANA
ALBANIA

SKOPJE

Pindus Mtns

GREECE

Aegean Sea

Dodecanese

Sicily

Marmot

Ionian Sea

Peloponnese

ATHENS

MALTA
VALLETTA

Mediterranean Sea

Crete

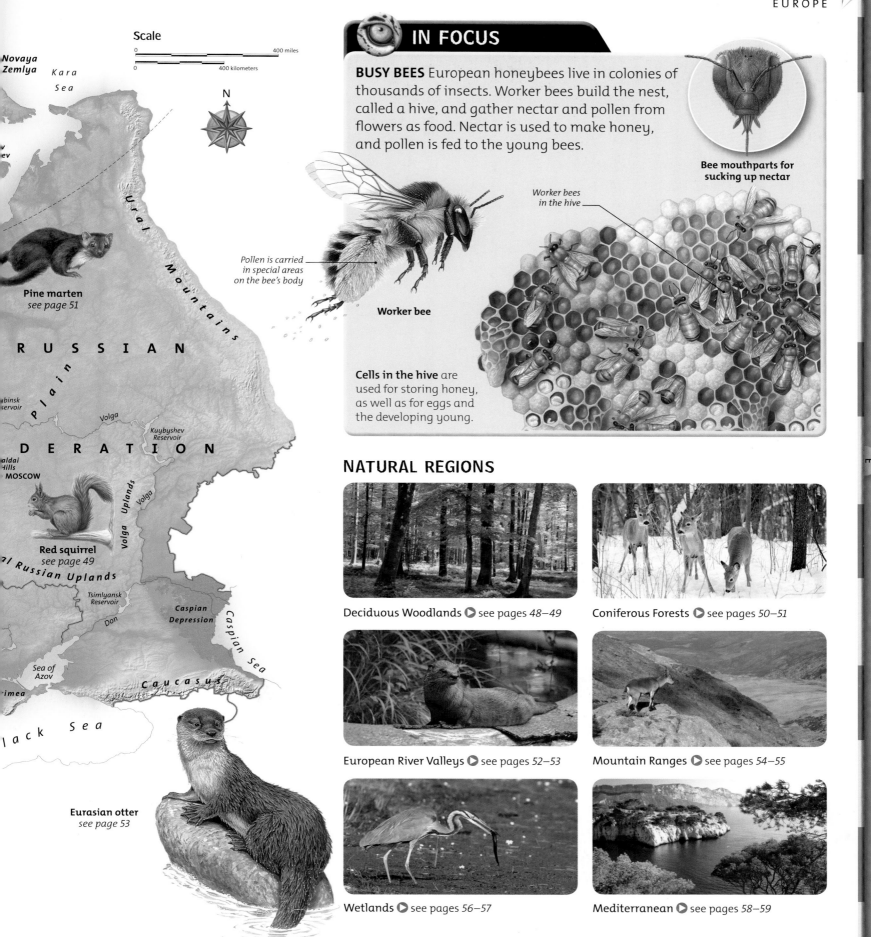

IN FOCUS

BUSY BEES European honeybees live in colonies of thousands of insects. Worker bees build the nest, called a hive, and gather nectar and pollen from flowers as food. Nectar is used to make honey, and pollen is fed to the young bees.

Bee mouthparts for sucking up nectar

Worker bees in the hive

Pollen is carried in special areas on the bee's body

Worker bee

Cells in the hive are used for storing honey, as well as for eggs and the developing young.

Pine marten *see page 51*

Red squirrel *see page 49*

Eurasian otter *see page 53*

NATURAL REGIONS

Deciduous Woodlands ▶ see pages 48–49

Coniferous Forests ▶ see pages 50–51

European River Valleys ▶ see pages 52–53

Mountain Ranges ▶ see pages 54–55

Wetlands ▶ see pages 56–57

Mediterranean ▶ see pages 58–59

Scale

Deciduous Woodlands

Blue tit

DECIDUOUS TREES are those that lose their leaves in the fall and grow fresh ones the following spring. Trees such as oak, beech, chestnut, and elm are some of the species found in the surviving areas of woodland in Europe. These provide food and shelter for many creatures. Birds and insects feed in the treetops on leaves and fruits, while on the woodland floor, ground birds, badgers, and rodents root around for food. Fall, when many of the trees produce nuts, is a plentiful time, allowing woodland animals to fatten up for the winter.

Woodland flowers
Spring blooms, such as bluebells, attract insects to the woodlands. They in turn are food for the migratory birds that return to Europe at this time of year.

Fallow deer
These deer usually live in separate herds of males and females. In the fall, males lock antlers in fierce fights to win mates.

Green woodpecker
This large, colorful woodpecker takes insects from tree trunks but also digs its beak into the ground to find ants. It laps these up with its long tongue.

The badger's excellent sense of smell helps it find food

European badger
Badgers live in family groups in underground dens called setts. They come out at night to feed. Earthworms are their favorite food, but they also eat insects, small mammals, and berries.

▶▶ FIT FOR LIFE

WOODLAND BUTTERFLIES Many of Europe's 576 kinds of butterflies live in woodlands, where there are plenty of leaves for their caterpillars to feed on.

Lesser purple emperor

Map butterfly

Camberwell beauty

Silver-washed fritillary

Red squirrel

Little owl

Black woodpecker

Badger

European mole

Wild boar
This fast-moving wild pig is the ancestor of domestic pigs. It usually feeds at night on anything from berries to small animals, and it can be surprisingly fierce if disturbed.

European jay
The jay's noisy, screeching call is a common sound in woodlands. It preys on smaller birds and their eggs, as well as on other animals.

The deciduous forest
One tree can support a wide range of wildlife. Squirrels and birds make nests in tree holes and find food on the branches and trunk. Soft earth beneath a tree makes it easier for burrowers, such as badgers and moles, to dig their homes.

IN DANGER! The red squirrel is common in much of Europe. In the UK and Italy, however, it is becoming rare because of competition from gray squirrels, introduced from the USA.

Coniferous Forests

Wood ant

WINTERS ARE LONG AND COLD in these northern European forests, but the cone-bearing trees, such as pine and spruce, are able to withstand the low temperatures. Their leaves are like tiny needles with little sap, so they do not freeze and are not shed in fall like the leaves of deciduous trees. Some large mammals, such as deer, manage to remain in the forests year-round, but many birds fly south for the winter. They return in the spring when insect life fills the forest, providing a welcome feast for birds and other creatures.

Barents Sea

Norwegian Sea

REYKJAVÍK

Ostersund

HELSINKI

OSLO · STOCKHOLM · TALLINN

North Sea

Baltic Sea

COPENHAGEN · RĪGA

VILNIUS

LONDON · AMSTERDAM

BRUSSELS · BERLIN · WARSAW

PARIS · PRAGUE · KIEV

BERN · VIENNA · BUDAPEST

BELGRADE · BUCHAREST

MADRID

ROME

Coniferous forest landscape
Few flowering plants can grow on the forest floor, where there is little light. Ferns do thrive, and moss and lichens grow on tree trunks.

Sharp talons are the long-eared owl's main weapon

Wildcat
A small number of wildcats live in Scottish coniferous forests. Larger than a domestic cat, this is a superb hunter with razor-sharp claws and powerful legs. A thick coat keeps it warm in the winter.

Long-eared owl
The tufts on this owl's head are just feathers, not ears. The real ears are hidden at the sides of the head. The owl preys on small mammals and birds.

Polecat

This member of the weasel family is a speedy hunter and climbs and swims well. It produces a strong scent from glands near its tail and uses this to warn off enemies and to mark its territory.

Antlers become more branched as the deer gets older

Whooper swans

These swans breed in the far north of Scandinavia and fly south to the UK and other parts of northern Europe for the winter. They feed on water plants, grass, and grain.

Red deer

The red deer is one of the largest land mammals in Europe. Males, called stags, can weigh up to 420 pounds (190 kg) and have highly branched antlers, which they shed and regrow each year.

Skillful climber

The pine marten also belongs to the weasel family. It hunts in the treetops as well as on the ground, and small mammals are its main prey.

IN FOCUS

DANCING GROUSE At the start of the breeding season, male black grouse perform displays to win females. They fan out their tail feathers and expand their red top knots as they strut to and fro in front of potential mates.

As they display, black grouse make a constant bubbling, cooing call.

European River Valleys

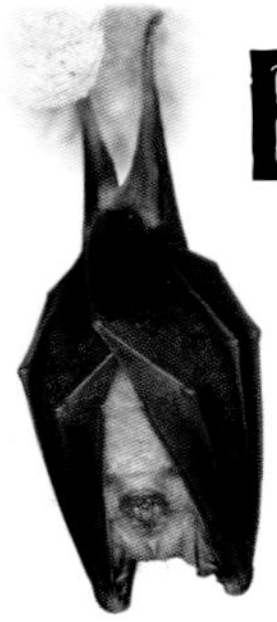

THE GREAT RIVERS of Europe have been seriously affected by dam building, farming, and industrial activity in recent years, but they are still home to plenty of fish, insects, birds, and other creatures. One of the most important river areas is the Coto Doñana in Spain. Its delta is now a national park, with marshes, dunes, and coastal lagoons inhabited by endangered species such as the Iberian lynx (*see page 46*) and the imperial eagle. It is well known for its bird life, and more than half of Europe's bird species can be seen here.

Horseshoe bat

River's edge

Shallow waters at the edges of rivers and ponds are a good feeding ground for long-legged wading birds, such as storks. The stork catches fish and other prey with its long beak.

▶▶▶ FIT FOR LIFE

BIG BEAKS A bird's beak is shaped according to the way it feeds. The heron uses its beak to stab at prey, while the spoonbill sifts through soft mud to find food. The curlew probes in the mud, and the flamingo filters tiny food items from the water.

Common spoonbill

Eurasian curlew

Purple heron

Greater flamingo

Home for wildlife

The Danube River contains 103 kinds of fish, more than half of all the freshwater species in Europe. This includes five species of sturgeons. Many birds and other animals visit its waters to find food or shelter along its banks.

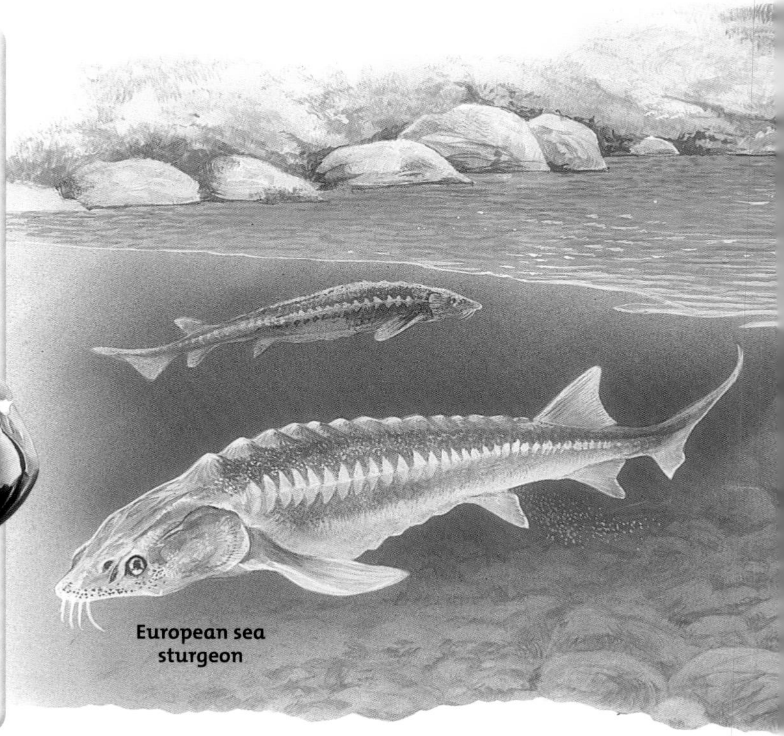

European sea sturgeon

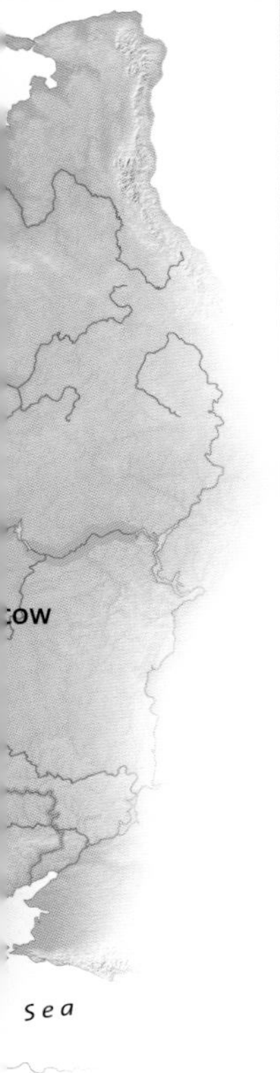

Eurasian otter

The sleek, streamlined otter is as at home in water as on land and swims with the aid of its webbed feet and strong tail. It catches fish, frogs, and crayfish, and it shelters in a den on a riverbank.

IN FOCUS

RIVER RODENTS These little rodents look like plump mice. They feed on plants and make burrows on riverbanks that have areas for nesting and food stores. Water voles are good swimmers.

Water vole

The bank vole eats insects, fruits, and birds' eggs as well as plants. It does not swim.

Common frog

This frog eats insects, worms, and snails, which it snaps up with its long, sticky tongue. In the winter, it buries itself in mud or dead leaves and hibernates.

Black stork

Common rabbit

Muskrat

Black stork

Souslik, or ground squirrel

Expert diver

The kingfisher is one of Europe's most colorful birds. It perches near water, watching for fish, then dives down to seize its prey in its long beak.

Sea

ow

Mountain Ranges

THE MOUNTAINS of Europe, from Sweden to Greece, are some of the wildest, least spoiled regions of this densely populated continent. The Alps is the largest of the European ranges. These mountains extend about 750 miles (1,200 km) and have a rich array of animal and plant species. Thanks to conservation measures, bears, wolves, and lynx are returning to these slopes, which are also home to animals such as marmots, chamois, and ibex. But the Alps and other European mountains are being affected by climate change, which could disrupt their ecosystems.

Red kite

N

Norwegian Sea

ATLANTIC OCEAN

North Sea

Baltic Sea

OSLO
STOCKHOLM
HELSINKI
TALLINN
RĪGA

DUBLIN
COPENHAGEN

VILNIUS

LONDON
AMSTERDAM
BERLIN
WARSAW

BRUSSELS

Bay of Biscay

PARIS
Ore Mtns.
PRAGUE

Salzburg
Carpathian Mountains
VIENNA

BERN
A l p s
BUDAPEST

Massif Central

Pyrenees

ZAGREB
Transylvanian Alps
BUCHAR

LISBON
MADRID
A p e n n i n e s
Dinaric Alps
BELGRADE

Sierra Morena
Balkan Mtns.

ROME
Rhodope Mtns.

M e d i t e r r a n e a n
Pindus Mtns.

S e a
ATHENS

W

S

Mountain goat

The ibex, a kind of wild goat, climbs the steepest slopes of the Alps with ease. It generally lives above the timberline.

Apollo butterfly

The Apollo butterfly was once common in alpine meadows at up to 6,400 feet (1,950 m), but it is now rarely seen. It feeds on flower nectar.

▶▶ FIT FOR LIFE

ADAPTING TO THE HEIGHTS
Mountain animals have thick coats to keep them warm at high altitudes, and they are very sure on their feet. Chamois have special flexible hooves that help them grip on rocky ground.

The nimble chamois can leap 6½ feet (2 m) high and as long as 20 feet (6 m).

The mouflon is a wild sheep. Males have much larger horns than females.

IN FOCUS

Watching for danger

MOUNTAIN DWELLERS Marmots belong to the squirrel family and live on many mountain ranges in Europe. They gather in large family groups and dig burrows for shelter. Plants are their main source of food, but marmots also eat insects and eggs.

Concealed entrance

Nesting chamber

Fresh grass for den

Griffon vulture
The griffon lives in southern Europe, where it soars over mountainous areas and rocky coasts searching for carrion. It rarely kills its own prey.

Eurasian lynx
This is the largest cat in Europe and one of the biggest predators, after bears and wolves. It has a thick coat, and in the winter it even grows fur on its feet to help it walk on snow.

Alpine newt
In the breeding season, the male alpine newt becomes more colorful and develops a crest along his back in order to attract females.

IN DANGER! The Pyrenean desman is a relative of moles, but it lives in mountain streams and is a good swimmer. It is now rare, mostly because of water pollution and habitat loss.

Wetlands

Dragonfly

ALL EUROPEAN COUNTRIES have some areas of wetland, which includes marshes, fens, bogs, peatlands, ponds, and coastal estuaries. The shaded areas on the map show the areas of greatest concentration of wetlands. They are vitally important habitats for wildlife, providing breeding grounds for fish and amphibians as well as food and shelter for many birds and other creatures. Some wetlands are constantly submerged. Others have seasonal flooding or are washed by daily tides.

N

Barents Sea

Norwegian Sea

OSLO
STOCKHOLM
HELSINKI
TALLINN

North Sea

DUBLIN
Cork
COPENHAGEN
RĪGA
MOSC

VILNIUS

LONDON
AMSTERDAM
BERLIN
WARSAW

BRUSSELS
KIEV

PARIS
PRAGUE

Bay of Biscay
BERN
VIENNA
BUDAPEST

BELGRADE
BUCHAREST

MADRID

ROME
Bla

Mediterranean Sea

ATLANTIC OCEAN

Baltic Sea

W

Wetland birds
Many birds, including wigeons and other ducks and geese, flock to wet grasslands and marshes to find food. They eat plants, such as marine eelgrass.

Marsh harrier

Life in a marshland
Marshland waters are rich in plant life and algae, which are eaten by fish, insects, and other small creatures. They in turn are food for birds and semiaquatic rodents, such as muskrats and water shrews.

Azure damselfly

▶▶▶ FIT FOR LIFE

SPECIAL BEAK The pied avocet has a very unusual upcurved beak that is ideal for its feeding method. The avocet stands in shallow, muddy water or marshland, swinging its beak from side to side like a scythe to find prey, such as worms, insects, and shellfish.

Smooth newt
This newt hunts on land and in water, catching prey such as insects, snails, and tadpoles. It lays its eggs in water and wraps them in the leaves of pond plants.

Poisonous shrew
The water shrew is a good swimmer and hunts for prey in water and on land. Its saliva contains a poison that helps it subdue larger victims.

Marsh frog
The largest European frog, this amphibian can be up to 6½ inches (17 cm) long. It spends much of its time in water and is a strong swimmer and jumper.

IN FOCUS

WATER INSECTS Marshes and wetlands are the perfect home for many kinds of water bugs and beetles. Some are good swimmers and hunt in water. Others, such as pond skaters and water striders, are light enough to run across the water surface.

The diving beetle traps a bubble of air between its wing cases and its abdomen, then uses this to breathe underwater.

The water boatman collects tiny plants with its front legs to eat and swims with its middle and back legs.

Purple heron

Muskrat

European perch

Water shrew

Mediterranean

Bearded vulture

ALMOST ENTIRELY SURROUNDED BY LAND, the Mediterranean Sea is only connected to the Atlantic Ocean by the narrow Strait of Gibraltar, between Africa and Spain. Its waters contain a huge range of creatures, many of which are unique, and its seagrass meadows are particularly rich in wildlife. Sadly, many of these creatures are becoming rare, due to overfishing, pollution, and other human pressures. The lands around the Mediterranean and its 5,000 islands are also home to many birds, reptiles, and other animals.

MADRID

Ligurian Sea

Corsica

ROME

Naples

Adriatic Sea

Majorca

Balearic Islands

Sardinia

Tyrrhenian Sea

Mediterranean

ALGIERS

Sicily

Ionia

TUNIS

Sea

Malta

AFRICA

Gulf of Sidra

Lesser-spotted dogfish

The waters of the Mediterranean are warmer and saltier than those of the Atlantic. There are at least 53 species of sharks here, including this dogfish.

Red star

This startlingly colorful sea star is one of the most common starfish in the Mediterranean. Its five arms are up to 7 inches (18 cm) long and can be regrown if lost or damaged.

▶▶ FIT FOR LIFE

REPTILES The warm, dry climate of Mediterranean lands is ideal for reptiles. More than 350 species live here, far more than in central and northern Europe. Almost half of these are found nowhere else.

Grass snake

Spur-thighed tortoise

The spur-thighed is one of four species of tortoises in this area. It lives in places with plenty of plant cover to hide in and feeds on leaves, fruits, and some carrion and dung.

Wall lizard

Gecko

N

W

S

Black Sea

Sea of Marmara

ASIA

ANKARA

Aegean Sea

Rhodes

Cyprus

BEIRUT

Crete

Sea

IN FOCUS

BARBARY MACAQUES These monkeys are the only wild primates living in Europe. A group was taken to Gibraltar in the 1700s, and there have been macaques there ever since. The monkeys forage for food on the ground and in trees during the day, eating leaves, roots, fruits, and insects.

Baby macaque

Bottlenose dolphin
Dolphins track fish in the sea with the help of echolocation. They make clicking sounds that bounce off prey back to the dolphin, revealing the prey's size and whereabouts.

Octopus
The octopus has a rounded body and eight arms, which are lined with suckers. It crawls over the seabed or swims headfirst, with arms trailing.

IN DANGER! The Mediterranean monk seal is one of the rarest mammals in the world. There are probably fewer than 400 left in the wild, and numbers are still falling, despite conservation efforts.

Squid
Like the octopus, the squid belongs to the mollusk group. It has a long body, eight arms, and two tentacles. It moves by shooting water out of its body to push itself along.

N

Africa

THIS HUGELY VARIED LAND has some of the world's most dramatic landscapes. Around the equator, where rainfall is regular and plentiful, are tropical forests, while to the north and south are vast grasslands and deserts. Many extraordinary animals live here, and Africa today has to balance the needs of its rapidly growing human population with the desire to protect its natural habitats and wildlife.

NATURAL REGIONS

Sahara and Sahel ▶ see pages 62–63

Congo Basin ▶ see pages 64–65

East African Savanna ▶ see pages 66–67

Miombo Woodlands ▶ see pages 68–69

Okavango Delta ▶ see pages 70–71

Kalahari ▶ see pages 72–73

Madagascar ▶ see pages 74–75

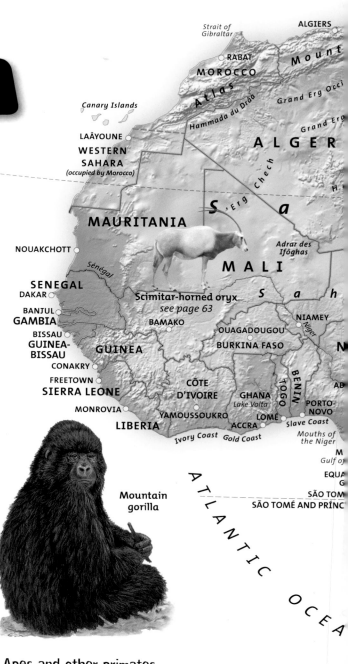

ALGIERS

Strait of Gibraltar

RABAT
MOROCCO

Mount

Atlas

Canary Islands

LAÂYOUNE
WESTERN SAHARA
(occupied by Morocco)

Hammāda du Drâa

Grand Erg Occi

Grand Erg

A L G E R

S'Erg Chech

MAURITANIA

NOUAKCHOTT

Adrar des Ifôghas

M A L I

Scimitar-horned oryx
see page 63

S a h

Sénégal

SENEGAL
DAKAR

BANJUL
GAMBIA

BAMAKO

NIAMEY

OUAGADOUGOU

BURKINA FASO

Niger

BISSAU
GUINEA-BISSAU

GUINEA

CONAKRY

FREETOWN
SIERRA LEONE

MONROVIA

CÔTE D'IVOIRE

GHANA
Lake Volta

TOGO

BENIN

PORTO-NOVO

YAMOUSSOUKRO

LOMÉ

ACCRA

Slave Coast

LIBERIA

Ivory Coast

Gold Coast

Mouths of the Niger

Gulf of

Mountain gorilla

EQUA

SÃO TOM
SÃO TOMÉ AND PRÍNC

A T L A N T I C   O C E A

Apes and other primates

Africa is home to all the great apes, apart from the orangutan, which lives in Asia. Gorillas, bonobos, and chimpanzees live here, as well as many kinds of baboons and other monkeys.

Mandrill   **Chimpanzee**   **Bonobo**   **Western gorilla**

W

S

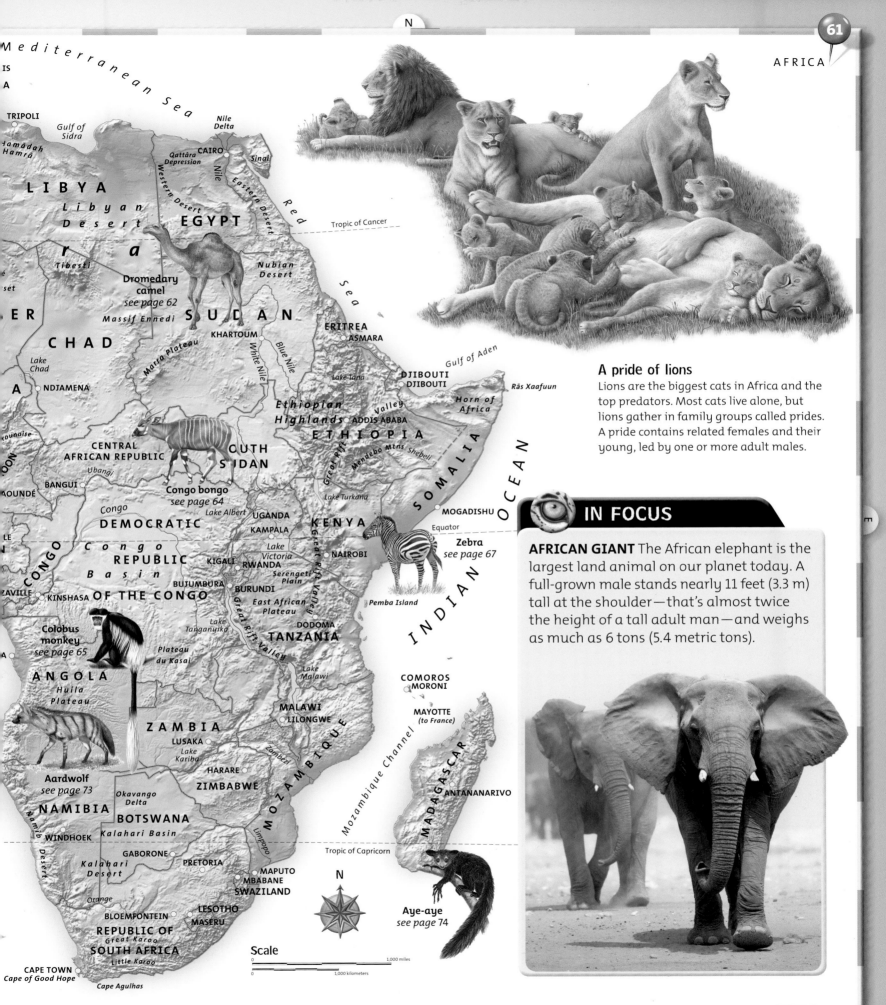

IS
A

Mediterranean Sea

TRIPOLI
Gulf of Sidra

Nile Delta

Ḥamādah el Ḥamrā'

Qattâra Depression CAIRO

Sinai

L I B Y A

Libyan Desert

Western Desert

Nile

Eastern Desert

E G Y P T

Tropic of Cancer

Red Sea

r a

Tibesti

Dromedary camel
see page 62

Massif Ennedi

S U D A N

Nubian Desert

KHARTOUM

Matra Plateau

White Nile

Blue Nile

ERITREA
ASMARA

é
set

Gulf of Aden

Rās Xaafuun

C H A D

Lake Chad

NDJAMENA

DJIBOUTI
DJIBOUTI

Lake Tana

Ethiopian Highlands

ADDIS ABABA

Horn of Africa

ETHIOPIA

Valley

rounaise

CENTRAL AFRICAN REPUBLIC

SOUTH SUDAN

Ubangi

Great Rift

Mendebo Mtns *Shebeli*

S O M A L I A

A

AOUNDÉ

BANGUI

Congo bongo
see page 64

Lake Turkana

Congo

Lake Albert

DEMOCRATIC

REPUBLIC

UGANDA
KAMPALA

KENYA

MOGADISHU

Equator

Congo Basin

Lake Victoria

NAIROBI

Zebra
see page 67

I N D I A N   O C E A N

ZAVILLE

KINSHASA

KIGALI
RWANDA

OF THE CONGO

BUJUMBURA
BURUNDI

Serengeti Plain

Great Rift Valley

Pemba Island

Colobus monkey
see page 65

Lake Tanganyika

East African Plateau

DODOMA

TANZANIA

Plateau du Kasai

IN FOCUS

ANGOLA

Huíla Plateau

Lake Malawi

COMOROS
MORONI

AFRICAN GIANT The African elephant is the largest land animal on our planet today. A full-grown male stands nearly 11 feet (3.3 m) tall at the shoulder—that's almost twice the height of a tall adult man—and weighs as much as 6 tons (5.4 metric tons).

ZAMBIA

MALAWI
LILONGWE

MAYOTTE
(to France)

LUSAKA
Lake Kariba

Zambezi

M O Z A M B I Q U E

HARARE

Aardwolf
see page 73

Okavango Delta

ZIMBABWE

NAMIBIA

BOTSWANA

WINDHOEK

Kalahari Basin

Namib Desert

Kalahari Desert

GABORONE

PRETORIA

ANTANANARIVO

M A D A G A S C A R

Mozambique Channel

Tropic of Capricorn

MAPUTO
MBABANE
SWAZILAND

Orange

Limpopo

Great Karoo

LESOTHO
MASERU

BLOEMFONTEIN

N

Aye-aye
see page 74

REPUBLIC OF SOUTH AFRICA

Little Karoo

CAPE TOWN
Cape of Good Hope

Cape Agulhas

Scale
0
1,000 miles
0
1,000 kilometers

E

A pride of lions

Lions are the biggest cats in Africa and the top predators. Most cats live alone, but lions gather in family groups called prides. A pride contains related females and their young, led by one or more adult males.

Sahara and Sahel

Jerboa

THE LARGEST HOT DESERT in the world, the Sahara covers an area almost the size of the United States. To its south is an area of dry grassland called the Sahel, which divides the desert from the tropical forests of central Africa. A surprising range of animals manage to live in the Sahara. Some escape the searing heat by sheltering in burrows. Others are able to go without water for many days.

N

Mediterranean Sea

ALGIERS
RABAT
Atlas Mountains
TRIPOLI
Gulf of Sirte
CAIRO
In Salah
Libyan Desert
Sahara
Western Desert
Nile
Tropic of Cancer
NOUAKCHOTT
Sahel
DAKAR
KHARTOUM
BAMAKO
NIAMEY
OUAGADOUGOU
NDJAMENA
YAMOUSSOUKRO
ABUJA
PORTO-NOVO
BANGUI

W

Desert dunes

Sand dunes cover vast areas of the Sahara, but there are also mountains and rocky lands. The Dorcas gazelle can survive without drinking and gets all the moisture it needs from the plants that it eats.

Water carrier

The sandgrouse has a clever way of taking water to its young. The male soaks his feathers in water, then flies back to the nest.

▶▶ FIT FOR LIFE

DESERT DWELLER The dromedary camel is well adapted for desert life and can live for several weeks without water. When it does drink, it can take in 30 gallons (114 L) in one session—as much as a bathful. Its wide, flat feet help it walk on sand, and its nostrils close to keep out dust.

Fat is stored in the hump and used when food is scarce

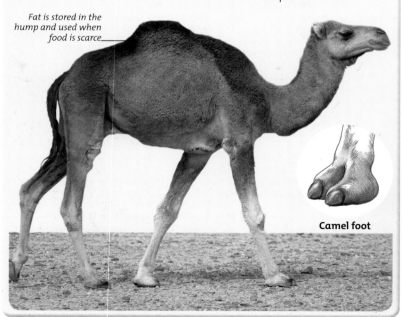

Camel foot

Egyptian vulture

Like other vultures, this bird feeds on dead animals, but it also likes to eat eggs. It throws stones at the eggs to break open their shells.

Pupa changes into an adult and then emerges from the ball

Larva becomes a pupa

Larva feeds inside the dung ball

S

IN FOCUS

DESERT WADI A wadi is an area of riverbed in the desert that is dry for most of the year but occasionally becomes flooded after a heavy rainfall. This allows plants to flourish briefly, and animals flock to the wadi to find food and drinking water.

Ostrich

Slender-horned
gazelles

Jerboa

Red-fronted
gazelles

Fennec fox
This is the smallest of all the foxes. Its coat merges well with the color of its surroundings, and its large ears help it lose heat and keep cool. It shelters in a burrow during the day and comes out at night to hunt.

Rock hyrax
These little creatures live on the scrubby land at the fringes of the Sahara, where they feed on grasses as well as insects and lizards. They are good climbers.

An egg is laid in the dung ball

Dung beetles
Dung beetles eat animal feces—dung—but also roll balls of dung and lay their eggs inside. The young hatch and grow in the dung ball.

IN DANGER! At one time, herds of scimitar-horned oryx lived in the Sahara, but now they are probably extinct in the wild. Fortunately, there are captive herds of these animals, and there are plans to reintroduce the oryx to the Sahara area.

Congo Basin

Gray parrot

THE TROPICAL FORESTS of the Congo Basin stretch thousands of miles across Central Africa. This is the second-largest tropical rainforest in the world and home to 1,000 kinds of birds and 400 mammal species, including three of the world's four great apes. But the great forest is under threat, and huge stretches have been destroyed already. Scientists are working with governments and local people to protect the Congo Basin—one of the most important of all remaining wild areas.

Life in the rainforest
Some of the rarest and most extraordinary of all African animals live in the Congo Basin. Their own survival depends on the survival of the rainforests.

Congo bongo
The bongo, one of the largest forest-living antelopes, usually feeds at night on forest plants. Both males and females have long horns.

Mighty apes
Gorillas are the largest of the primates. They live in family groups led by an adult male, often known as a silverback because of the light hair on his back.

Okapi
The okapi is related to giraffes, not zebras, despite its stripy back legs. It lives in the heart of the forest and was only discovered by scientists in 1901. Leaves and fruits are its main food.

Colobus monkey

This acrobatic monkey spends nearly all its time high in the trees. Its specially adapted stomach allows it to eat leaves that are toxic to other monkeys.

Ross's turaco

Flocks of these birds live in the forest canopy, where they feed on plants and fruits as well as some insects. The long tail helps the turaco balance as it hops from branch to branch.

Gaboon viper

This snake lies almost hidden among leaves on the forest floor, ready to strike and kill small creatures such as mice, birds, and frogs.

Wild pig

The red river hog lives in herds of as many as 40 animals that roam the forest feeding on plants, insects, and other animals. It uses its long strong snout to root around on the ground for food.

IN DANGER! The pygmy hippopotamus is only active at night and is rarely seen. This animal has probably never been common but is now endangered.

IN FOCUS

COLORFUL MONKEYS Mandrills are the largest monkeys. They live in family groups led by a dominant male, which has the brightest face markings. The monkeys find most of their food—fruits, roots, and small animals—on the ground, but they sleep in the trees.

Grooming one another helps keep members of the group close.

A mandrill's face markings become even brighter when the animal is excited.

East African Savanna

Thompson's gazelle

THE TROPICAL GRASSLANDS of East Africa are now the only place in the world where huge herds of grazing animals are still found. Here live wildebeests, zebras, gazelles, impalas, and giraffes—as well as the predators that follow them. The grass survives, despite all the animals, because it grows from its base, so it keeps on pushing upward no matter how many times the tips are eaten. It is hot all year long here, but there is a dry season and a wet season. The timing of the rainy season varies over the region.

The great migration

Twice a year, more than a million wildebeests and many other animals follow the rains and trek across the savanna in search of fresh grass to eat.

Lappet-faced vulture

The biggest African vulture, this bird has a large and powerful beak. It is often the first to arrive at a carcass and tear it open. It also kills its own prey.

Long-necked gerenuks

These slender gazelles can stand on their hind legs for long periods while they feed. This means they can eat leaves on branches that are too high for other antelopes to reach.

Map labels: KHARTOUM, ASMARA, NDJAMENA, Lake Tana, DJIBOUTI, ADDIS ABABA, BANGUI, YAOUNDÉ, Lake Turkana, MOG, LIBREVILLE, KAMPALA, Equato, KIGALI, Lake Victoria, Masai Mara, NAIROBI, BRAZZAVILLE, KINSHASA, BUJUMBURA, Serengeti Plain, IND, DODOMA, OCEA, LUANDA, MORONI, LILONGWE, LUSAKA, Red Sea, Gulf

A giraffe's long neck contains only 7 neck bones (vertebrae), just like a human's

IN FOCUS

TERMITE TOWERS These mounds dot the savanna and are home to millions of insects called termites. The top is a kind of air-conditioning system to keep the temperature steady, and below are chambers for young and food stores.

Chimney for taking warm air out of the nest

Areas for growing fungus, used as food

Royal chamber for queen termite

Tallest land animals

A giraffe can be up to 19 feet (5.8 m) tall, so it is able to see across the plains and watch out for predators. Its strong tongue is an amazing 20 inches (50 cm) long—ideal for grasping treetop leaves.

The queen termite is much larger than the others, and she is the only one that lays eggs—up to 2,000 a day.

Zebras

A zebra's stripes are unique—no two animals have exactly the same pattern. Zebras live in large herds and roam the savanna, feeding mostly on tall grasses.

Speedy cat

The cheetah is the world's fastest land animal. It can run up to 68 miles an hour (109 km/h) as it chases its prey across the savanna. Its long tail helps it balance as it runs.

Snake eater

The long-legged secretary bird can fly and run fast. It catches snakes, which it kills by stomping on them with its strong feet.

Miombo Woodlands

Greater kudu

DENSE FOREST and grassland cover this large area of south-central Africa, which is home to a wide range of wildlife, including lions, rhinoceroses, and chimpanzees, as well as many kinds of birds. Temperatures are high all year long, and there is a long dry season, when animals gather around any available waterholes. Nearly all the rain falls during the summer months, from November to March. The name Miombo comes from the local name for one of the most common trees in the area.

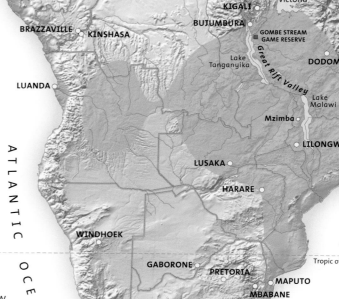

Rich plant life
At least 8,500 kinds of plants grow in these woodlands, and as many as half of these grow nowhere else. The trees provide cover for many animals, including lions.

Ground pangolin
The pangolin tears open ant and termite nests with its strong claws, then laps up the insects with its long tongue.

Large scales protect the body

Tree dwellers
Vervet monkeys are common in these woodlands and spend most of their time in the trees, eating leaves and shoots, sleeping, and grooming.

Nile crocodile
This animal is one of the fiercest predators in Africa. It hunts anything it can find, from fish to wildebeests—and even people! It grows up to 16 feet (5 m) long and weighs as much as three adult humans.

Powerful jaws are lined with 64 to 68 teeth

Tough skin is studded with plates of bone

Northern carmine bee-eater

This bird snatches bees and wasps from the air with its slender beak, then bangs its catch against a branch to remove the sting before eating.

Wattled crane

The wattle—fleshy skin—that dangles from its throat gives this bird its name. It feeds on water plants, as well as frogs and insects, and plunges its head into water when feeding.

IN DANGER! Demand for rhinoceros horn for traditional medicine has resulted in the black rhinoceros becoming critically endangered. However, strict protection is leading to a slight rise in numbers.

Elephant families

Female elephants and their young live in family groups led by a dominant female. Males wander alone or with other males and join the females only for mating.

Puff adder

This large snake grows to more than 6 feet (1.8 m) long and is a powerful predator. It lies in wait for small animals and kills them with its venomous bite.

IN FOCUS

MAKING FACES Chimpanzees show their feelings in their facial expressions. They have more expressions than any other animal, except humans. Chimps are our closest relatives and share 98 percent of our DNA.

Playful   Aggressive   Attentive

Hungry   Submissive   Frightened

Tool user

Chimpanzees are highly intelligent animals and sometimes use tools to help them get food. They poke sticks into insect nests, use stones to open nuts, and soak up drinking water with leaves.

Okavango Delta

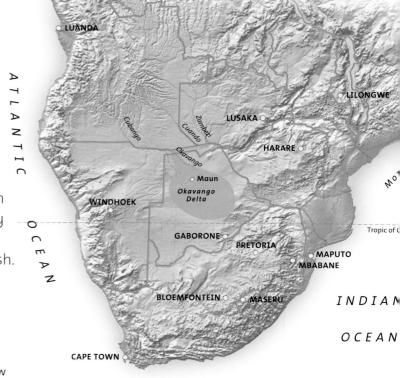

Warthog

THE LARGEST INLAND DELTA in the world, the Okavango is an extraordinary natural region in the heart of Africa. It is 6,000 square miles (15,500 km^2) of channels, lagoons, and islands. Normally rivers flow into the sea, but the Okavango River ends in a huge floodplain that fans out across northern Botswana. The delta changes throughout the year, shrinking back in the dry season and expanding again when the rains swell the river. This watery wilderness is a wonderful refuge for animals and home to hippopotamuses, at least 400 kinds of birds, and millions of fish.

Red lechwe
This antelope is slow on land but can run surprisingly fast in water. Its speed in water is due to its strong hindquarters and its long, splayed hooves.

Hippopotamus highways
Huge hippos create ever-changing channels and waterways between lakes as they bulldoze their way through the swamps. Many other kinds of animals, including cranes, mongooses, and otters, live and feed in these swamps.

IN FOCUS

EXPERT CLIMBER The leopard is one of the most agile of all big cats. It is also extremely strong. It often drags its prey up into the branches of a tree, where it can eat in peace, without disturbance from scavengers, such as hyenas.

Leopard watching for prey

Leopards catch large animals such as antelopes and warthogs, as well as monkeys, hares, and hyraxes.

Papyrus

Cape clawless otter

Water cabbage

Water crane

Marsh mongoose

Water lilies

▶▶ FIT FOR LIFE

HEAVY HIPPO The hippopotamus is the heaviest land animal after the elephant. It weighs as much as 8,000 pounds (3,600 kg)—more than two small cars. It spends the day in water to keep cool, then comes on to land at night to feed on plants.

A hippo's biggest teeth are about 18 inches (45 cm) long and very sharp.

Hippos live in groups of females and young, led by a male. He defends them against other males.

Water antelope
The sitatunga is well adapted to swamp life. Its splayed hooves help it walk on soft, muddy ground, and its oily coat is water resistant. It swims well and can dive to escape danger.

African buffalo
Both male and female buffalo have large horns. These make handy perches for oxpeckers and other birds that seize and eat insects from the buffalo's coat.

Cape clawless otter
The cape otter handles prey with its front feet, which have no claws or webbing and look like human hands. It does have claws on two toes of each back foot.

Hammerhead stork

African fish-eagle
This eagle perches above water to watch for fish near the surface. It then swoops down with its feet held forward to grab its victim.

Hippopotamus

IN DANGER! African wild dogs are pack hunters and kill animals much larger than themselves. Many have been shot by farmers or died from disease spread from domestic animals, and they are now endangered.

Kalahari

Citrus swallowtail butterfly

ALTHOUGH EXTREMELY DRY, the Kalahari is not a true desert. Most of this large area of land in southern Africa is flat and high, about 3,000 feet (915 m) above sea level. Some is covered with endless dunes, but there is also scrub, acacia woodland, and even areas of grassland, particularly after rainfall. Many of the animals that live here have become adapted to life with little water and can survive during long periods without rain.

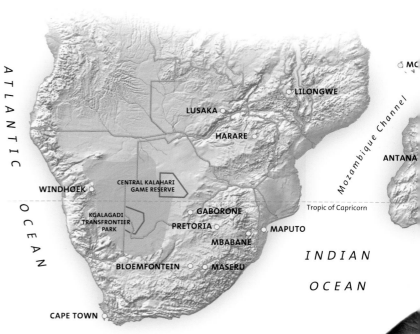

Life without water
Gemsbok are large, long-horned antelopes that manage to survive on the coarse grasses that grow in the Kalahari. They also eat roots and bulbs for their water content.

Springbok
Grass is the main food of this antelope, but in the Kalahari, it also eats wild melons for their water content and can survive for long periods without drinking.

Leopard tortoise
This beautifully marked tortoise thrives in these dry lands, where it feeds on plants such as prickly pears and thistles.

Meerkat families
Meerkats are a kind of mongoose and live in groups of 50 or so animals. They work together to find food and keep one another safe, a few keeping watch while others hunt or care for young. If one animal calls the alarm, all dive into their burrows.

IN DANGER! The southern ground hornbill lives in groups of up to eight, but only the leading pair lay eggs. The rest help rear the young. Many of these hornbills have been killed by hunters, and they are now rare.

Kalahari lions

Even the mighty lion adapts to life in the Kalahari. Lions here live in smaller groups than elsewhere, and they hunt smaller prey.

Termite hunter

The aardwolf is a kind of hyena but has a very different diet from the rest of its family. It lives mostly on termites and may eat up to 200,000 in one night.

▶▶▶ FIT FOR LIFE

INSECT EATER The aardvark is built for insect eating. It tears open termite and ant nests with its strong claws. It then sticks its long snout into the nest and laps up the fleeing insects with its sticky tongue, which is up to 12 inches (30 cm) long.

Its thick, almost hairless skin protects the aardvark from the bites and stings of its insect prey.

Speedy bird

The ostrich is the largest of all birds and the fastest runner. It can sprint at up to 43 miles an hour (70 km/h). It gets most of the water it needs from its plant food.

Madagascar

Golden mantella frog

THIS TROPICAL ISLAND IN THE INDIAN OCEAN is about the size of Texas and home to more than 250,000 kinds of animals. An amazing 80 percent of these are found nowhere else on Earth. Madagascar is the world's fourth-largest island and also the oldest; it was created when the great southern continent broke apart more than 160 million years ago. Since then, the island's wildlife has evolved in complete isolation, resulting in this collection of rare and unique creatures.

N

Tanjona Bobaomby

Antsiranana

Nosy Bé
Lohatanjona Angadoka

BORA
SPECIAL RESERVE

Mahajanga

Tanjona Vilanandro

ANKARAFANTSIKA
NATURE RESERVE

Helodrano Antongila

Tanjona M

Nosy Boraha

Toamasina

○ **ANTANANARIVO**

Madagascar

INDIAN

Fianarantsoa

OCEAN

Tanjona Ankaboa

Toliara ○ .... Tropic of Capricorn

Tanjona Vohimena

M
o
z
a
m
b
i
q
u
e

C
h
a
n
n
e
l

A divided island

A range of mountains runs the length of Madagascar, dividing the island in two. To the east is dense jungle, and to the west and south are areas of drier forest and thorny desert.

Extra-long third finger on each hand

Parson's chameleon

About half of all the world's chameleon species live in Madagascar. Like its relatives, Parson's chameleon catches its insect prey with a lightning-fast strike of its long, sticky tongue.

Aye-aye

This lemur hunts by tapping on a tree branch and listening for insects moving under the bark. It then pulls out the prey with its long fingers.

Feet are shaped for holding onto branches

The tongue is up to twice the length of the chameleon's body

Hissing cockroaches live only in Madagascar

W

S

IN FOCUS

LEAPING LEMURS Lemurs are primates, like monkeys and apes, and live only on the island of Madagascar. There are about 80 different kinds, ranging from tiny mouse lemurs to larger ring-tailed lemurs, sifakas, and indris. All have grasping hands and feet and are skilled climbers and leapers.

Red-ruffed lemur

Gray mouse lemur

Red-bellied lemur

Ring-tailed lemur

Rufous-headed ground roller

The roller is found only in Madagascar, where it lives in the rainforest and feeds on insects. It nests in holes in the ground.

IN DANGER! The fossa is the largest carnivore in Madagascar. It might look like a cat, but it is a relative of the mongoose. Little is known about this dagger-toothed creature, and it is thought to be increasingly rare.

Helmet vanga

This large-beaked bird lives in the forest in the northeast part of the island. It snaps up insects and other creatures from branches and the ground.

Coquerel's sifaka

The sifaka, a type of lemur, leaps gracefully from tree to tree with the help of its long legs and tail. On the ground, it stands upright and bounds along on its back legs.

Giant leaf-tailed gecko

The coloring of this lizard makes it almost invisible as it lies sleeping on the bark of a tree during the day. It hunts insects at night.

N

Asia

The Asian elephant is smaller than its African cousin but still the largest Asian land animal

ASIA IS THE WORLD'S LARGEST continent by far. It stretches from beyond the Arctic Circle to south of the equator and includes many kinds of landscapes, from the frozen wastes of Siberia to the hot, wet forests of Southeast Asia. It has the world's highest mountain, as well as some of the coolest, wettest, and driest places on Earth. Asia is also home to an extraordinary range of creatures, such as tigers, giant pandas, and orangutans; plus, new animal species are still being discovered there.

White-backed vulture

This vulture was once one of the most common birds of prey in Asia, but it is now very rare. Many birds died after eating the bodies of animals that had been treated with a particular veterinary drug.

Saiga
see page 81

Giant pand
see page 9

Black bear
see page 84

RUSSIAN FE

N

TURKEY
ANKARA
GEORGIA
NICOSIA
CYPRUS
T'BILISI
ARMENIA
YEREVAN
AZERBAIJAN
LEBANON
BEIRUT
ISRAEL
SYRIA
DAMASCUS
JERUSALEM
AMMAN
JORDAN
IRAQ
BAGHDAD
BAKU
TEHRAN
ASTANA
KAZAKHSTAN
UZBEKISTAN
TASHKENT
TURKMENISTAN
ASHGABAT
BISHKEK
KYRGYZSTAN
DUSHANBE
TAJIKISTAN
IRAN
KUWAIT
KUWAIT
SAUDI
ARABIA
RIYADH
BAHRAIN
QATAR
DOHA
ABU DHABI
UNITED ARAB
EMIRATES
MUSCAT
OMAN
SAN'A
YEMEN
KABUL
AFGHANISTAN
ISLAMABAD
PAKISTAN
NEW
DELHI
NEPAL
KATHMANDU
THIMPHU
BHUTAN
BANGLADESH
DACCA
C H
INDIA
SRI LANKA
COLOMBO
MALE
MALDIVES
Maldives

Kara Sea
Ural Mountains
West Siberian Plain
Caspian Depression
Kazakhskiy Plain
Aral Sea
Ustyurt Plateau
Turan Lowland
Lake Balkhash
Altai Mountains
Tien Shan
Tarim Basin
Taklimakan Desert
Kunlun Shan
Plateau of Tibet
Himalaya
Black Sea
Anatolia
Caucasus
Caspian Sea
Karakum Desert
Hindu Kush
Iranian Plateau
Zagros
Syrian Desert
An Nafud
Red Sea
Arabian Peninsula
Rub'al Khali
Gulf of Aden
Socotra
Arabian Sea
Gulf of Oman
Persian Gulf
Indus
Thar Desert
Gangetic Plain
Ganges
Indian Subcontinent
Deccan Plateau
Western Ghats
Eastern Ghats
Bay of Bengal
Laccadive Islands
Laccadive Sea
Andaman Islands
Nicobar Islands
I N D I A N   O C E A N
ARC
Severnaya Zemlya
Nort

IN FOCUS

VENOMOUS LIZARD The Komodo dragon is the world's heaviest lizard and grows up to 10 feet (3 m) long. It attacks large prey, killing with its venomous bite. Even if the victim escapes, it slowly dies from the venom, and the Komodo then feasts on its body.

The Komodo's feet are equipped with strong, sharp claws.

Fruit bat
see page 93

Scale

0 — 750 miles

0 — 750 kilometers

Chukchi Sea

Wrangel Island

Bering Strait

Gulf of Anadyr

East Siberian Sea

Bering Sea

Siberian Islands

Lena

Verkhoyanskiy Khrebet

Momskiy Khrebet

Khrebet Cherskogo

Kamchatka Peninsula

Sea of Okhotsk

Siberian tiger
see page 79

Sakhalin

Kuril Islands

Heilong Jiang (Amur)

Argun

Sikhote Alin

Hokkaidō

Onager
see page 82

Manchurian Plain

Sea of Japan

ULAANBAATAR

BEIJING

NORTH KOREA
P'YŎNGYANG

Korea Bay
SEOUL
SOUTH KOREA

Bo Hai

Yellow

Korean Peninsula

JAPAN
TOKYO
Honshū

Shikoku

Kyūshū

Korea Strait

Yellow Sea

Great Plain of China

Yangtze

East China Sea

Ryukyu Islands

Clouded leopard
see page 88

Taiwan Strait

Tropic of Cancer

TAIPEI
TAIWAN

P A C I F I C   O C E A N

HANOI

Hainan

Luzon

Philippine Sea

VIENTIANE

South China Sea

Indochina Peninsula

VIETNAM

CAMBODIA

MANILA

Mindoro

Philippines
Samar

PHILIPPINES

Panay

Negros *Cebu*

Palawan

Mindanao

Sulu Sea

BANDAR SERI BEGAWAN
BRUNEI

Celebes Sea

Malay Peninsula

MALAYSIA
KUALA LUMPUR

SINGAPORE
SINGAPORE

Greater Sunda Islands

Borneo

Sulawesi

Moluccas

New Guinea

INDONESIA

Malay Archipelago

Java Sea

Flores Sea

Banda Sea

Arafura Sea

JAKARTA

Java

Lesser Sunda Islands

DILI
EAST TIMOR

Timor Sea

NATURAL REGIONS

Siberia ▶ see pages 78–79

Steppe ▶ see pages 80–81

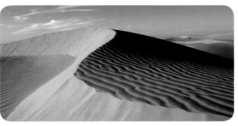

Hot and Cold Deserts ▶ see pages 82–83

The Himalayas ▶ see pages 84–85

Indian Subcontinent ▶ see pages 86–87

Lower Mekong ▶ see pages 88–89

Mountains of Southwest China
▶ see pages 90–91

Rainforests of Southeast Asia
▶ see pages 92–93

Staying warm
Japanese macaques live farther north than any other nonhuman primates. One way that they keep warm in the winter is by bathing in the waters of hot springs.

Siberia

HUGE FORESTS cover much of this northern land—one of the world's last great wildernesses. These taiga forests, as they are known, contain coniferous trees, such as larch, spruce, and pine, and provide shelter for many creatures, including grouse, brown bears, and wolverines. To the north of the taiga is the tundra, an area of polar desert, where summers are short and winters long and very cold. Trees cannot grow in these harsh conditions, but there are small bushes, and grasses and lichens carpet the ground.

Hazel grouse

N

ARCTIC OCEAN

Kara Sea

Laptev Sea

East Siberian Sea

Lena

Verkhoyansk

Yenisey

Arctic Circle

Sea of Okhotsk

Lake Baikal

○ **ASTANA**

ULAANBAATAR ○

Sea of Japan

BISHKEK

BEIJING ○ **P'YŎNGYANG** **SEOUL**

Yellow Sea

East China Sea

W

S

Siberian bears
Siberian brown bears hibernate in the winter when temperatures plummet. In the spring, they emerge and may travel long distances in search of food.

Slightly hooked beak is ideal for picking berries

Siberian jay
This little bird is common in Siberian forests but moves closer to villages in the winter to find food scraps. It makes its nest in a conifer tree and lays four eggs.

Waxwing
Berries are the main source of food for this bird, but it also eats insects. Waxwings breed in the taiga and make a nest lined with grass and moss in a pine or spruce tree.

Ural owl
Like most owls, the Ural owl hunts at night, swooping down on victims such as voles, hares, and frogs. It nests in tree holes and lays three or four eggs each year.

Ears are hidden in the feathers at the sides of the head. Owls have excellent hearing

Feathers have soft edges to help the owl fly silently and surprise prey

IN FOCUS

FRESHWATER SEALS Baikal seals are the smallest of all seals. They live in the icy waters of the world's deepest lake—Siberia's Lake Baikal. The seals feed mostly on fish, which they catch during dives lasting 40 minutes or more. In the winter, the lake is covered with ice, and the seals claw holes in the ice where they can come to breathe.

Largest tiger
The Siberian tiger is the largest tiger and the biggest big cat. It is strictly protected, but there are now believed to be fewer than 500 individuals left in the wild.

Winter sleep
The Arctic ground squirrel eats as much as it can in the summer and almost doubles its weight. In the winter, it escapes the cold by hibernating in an underground burrow.

Snowy owl
Only mature male snowy owls are pure white. Females and young birds have some dark markings. The owls live on the tundra, and lemmings are their favorite prey.

Sable
A relative of the weasel, the sable lives in the taiga forest, where it hunts birds and small mammals. It is still hunted for its thick fur, which protects it from the cold.

IN DANGER! The Siberian crane is critically endangered, mostly due to hunting and loss of habitat. The birds breed in Siberia, then fly south to spend the winter in Iran, India, or China.

Steppe

Gerbil

IN CENTRAL ASIA, there is a vast area of steppe, or grassland, amid the foothills of the great mountain ranges. In this rugged land, hot, windy, dry summers are followed by cold winters, so this is not an easy home for wildlife. Most common are grazing animals, such as antelopes, and small burrowing mammals. The burrowers, such as hamsters, are a source of food for hunters, including foxes and birds of prey.

High steppes

Winters are severe on the high steppe. Any surface water freezes and there are only low-growing plants, so there are few places for animals to find shelter.

Przewalski's horse

Herds of these horses used to roam the steppe, but they became extinct in the wild. Horses bred in captivity have now been released into the area.

Goitered gazelle

This speedy gazelle can run at 35 miles per hour (56 km/h). Only males have horns, and they also have swollen throats during the breeding season.

GROUND DWELLERS Lots of little rodents, such as ground squirrels, hamsters, and voles, shelter in burrows on the steppe. They pop up to the surface to find food.

Steppe lemmings are usually active at night, when they feed on leaves and seeds. They do not hibernate.

Black-bellied hamsters store food in their burrows. They hibernate in the winter, waking up every few days to feed.

Corsac fox

This fox is well adapted to its dry habitat and can go for long periods without food and water. It preys on ground squirrels, marmots, and other small mammals and will take over and enlarge their burrows for shelter.

Steppe eagle

This powerful bird of prey often soars above the steppe searching for prey but also hunts on the ground. Susliks, a type of ground squirrel, are its main source of food.

Pallas's cat

Pallas's cat, also known as the manul, lives alone and takes shelter in caves and rock crevices. It is about the size of a big domestic cat and hunts rodents and other small prey.

Great bustard

The male great bustard can be twice the size of a female, and at more than 35 pounds (16 kg), it is probably the heaviest of all flying birds.

IN DANGER! The saiga is an unusual antelope with a large, trunklike nose. Huge herds once grazed on the steppe, but numbers have declined due to uncontrolled hunting.

Hot and Cold Deserts

Sunspider

SAND DUNES, barren mountains, and rocky, pebbly ground cover the huge desert regions of central Asia. Temperatures vary from searing heat to freezing cold, and there is very little rain—generally less than 10 inches (25 cm) a year. Only low-growing tough plants can survive, and animals must adapt to life with little drinking water. Many animals burrow underground to escape the cold or heat and only come to the surface to feed.

Map labels: N, ULAANBAATAR, TASHKENT, BISHKEK, Dalanzadgad, *Karakum Desert*, DUSHANBE, *Gobi Desert*, *Taklimakan Desert*, KABUL, ISLAMABAD, *Thar Desert*, NEW DELHI, KATHMANDU, THIMPHU, Tropic of Cancer, DACCA, HANOI, *Bay of Bengal*, VIENTIANE, RANGOON, BANGKOK, PHNOM PENH, W, S

Cold deserts

Temperatures drop to −40°F (−40°C) in the Gobi Desert during the winter. The Gobi is the largest Asian desert and covers an area of about 500,000 square miles (1,300,000 km²).

Fat is stored in the humps and can be used as food when needed

Thick fur keeps the camel warm in the winter

IN DANGER! The onager, or wild ass, is one of the fastest-running members of the horse family. It is now rare and lives in only two protected areas, but these animals are still at risk from poachers.

Long-eared hedgehog

True to its name, this hedgehog has much larger ears than other hedgehogs, possibly to help it lose heat. It hunts at night, catching insects and other small creatures.

Bactrian camel

Bactrians are now the only wild camels and are extremely rare—there are fewer than 1,000 left. The camels shed their thick coat in the summer.

Two toes spread wide to help the camel walk on sand

ASIA

Sea of
Japan

P'YŎNGYANG
SEOUL
TOKYO

Yellow
Sea

East China
Sea

TAIPEI

Cinereous vulture

This vulture is the biggest bird of prey in Asia. It rarely kills its own prey, and it feeds mostly on carrion, which it tears apart with its large beak.

Desert hunter

The golden eagle is a superb hunter. It soars high over these vast barren lands searching for prey, then dives down to seize its victim in its powerful talons.

Gray's monitor

The Gray's monitor shelters in a burrow at night and comes out to hunt in the morning. It uses its sensitive forked tongue to track down prey such as small mammals and insects.

Hot deserts

The Thar Desert in India is the world's seventh-largest desert. The winters here are cold, but the summers are very hot, with a small amount of rain between July and September.

Central Asian pit viper

Like all pit vipers, this snake has a special sensory pit on each side of its head. These detect heat to help the snake find warm-blooded prey, such as mice, at night.

IN FOCUS

DESERT BURROWERS Jerboas leap over the desert sands like tiny kangaroos on their extra-long back legs. They live in burrows to shelter from the heat in the summer and cold in the winter and come out at night to feed. Leaves, roots, and seeds are their main diet, and jerboas get all the water they need from their food.

A jerboa's burrow is about 3 feet (90 cm) long and includes a sleeping area that is lined with plants or animal hair.

Lebetine viper

This desert-living snake grows up to 6 feet (1.8 m) long and has a highly venomous bite. It is active at night and at dusk and dawn and hunts rodents and birds.

The Himalayas

Bhutan glory butterfly

THIS GREAT MOUNTAIN RANGE extends about 1,490 miles (2,400 km) between the Indian subcontinent and Tibet. Snow and ice cover many of its peaks all year long, including the highest, Mount Everest. At 29,035 feet (8,850 m), Everest is the world's highest mountain. Most animals live on the lower slopes of the range, and these creatures have become adapted to the craggy land and the cold climate. Some have thick fur to keep them warm. Others, such as marmots, hibernate through the harsh winter weather.

Alarm call
Marmots belong to the squirrel family. They live and feed in groups, and if one marmot spots danger, it makes an alarm call so all can dive for cover.

Markhor
The markhor is a wild goat with large corkscrew horns. Males have much larger horns than females and use these in fierce battles to win mates during the breeding season.

IN DANGER! The Himalayan black bear climbs to heights of 15,000 feet (4,500 m) in the summer and feeds on nuts and honey as well as insects and larger animals. The bear has suffered from loss of habitat and poaching and is now rare.

Himalayan tahr
This skillful climber usually stays on high slopes, at altitudes of 15,000 feet (4,500 m), all year round. It feeds on grass in the summer and mosses and ferns in the winter.

Mountain monkeys
Beautiful golden langurs live in the treetops in forests in the Himalayan foothills. There are only about 5,000 left in the wild.

Himalayan yak
The largest of the Himalayan herbivores is the yak, which lives on treeless plateaus, feeding on grass and lichens. Its shaggy coat keeps it warm.

Himalayan musk deer
This deer has no antlers but does have big canine teeth. Its dense coat helps keep it warm, and its wide hooves allow it to clamber on steep, rocky slopes.

Monal pheasant
Male monals have much more colorful plumage than females. They show off their finery in courtship dances.

👁 IN FOCUS

MOUNTAIN CAT The snow leopard is an amazingly agile big cat, able to chase prey such as mountain sheep and goats over rocky crags and peaks. Its tail is almost as long as its body and used to help it balance as well as to wrap around itself for warmth. Like most cats, it lives alone, except when breeding.

Gray markings help camouflage the snow leopard among rocky slopes.

The thick fur is nearly 5 inches (12 cm) long on the snow leopard's underside.

Western tragopan
Like most pheasants, the tragopan spends most of its time on the ground feeding on leaves, seeds, and insects.

Indian Subcontinent

Gaur

INDIA AND ITS NEIGHBORS lie on the same plate of Earth's crust. The area, sometimes referred to as South Asia, is huge but not large enough to be termed a separate continent—hence the name subcontinent. The climate of most of the region is dominated by monsoons, with heavy rains and storms in the summer and drier, cooler weather in the winter. There is a wide range of habitats, including tropical forests and vast wetlands around the Ganges and Indus rivers.

Indian monkeys
Common, or Hanuman, langurs are the most widespread monkeys in India. They live everywhere, from the Himalayan foothills to tropical forests and deserts.

The cobra can raise a third of its body up off the ground

Useful trunks
Asian elephants feed on plant matter such as leaves, grasses, tree bark, and fruits. An elephant can use its trunk to do anything, from tearing up trees to plucking a tiny leaf.

Expert climber
The Asian palm civet lives mostly in the trees, where it eats fruits and buds as well as insects and other small animals. It is usually active at night.

Map labels:
N
TASHKENT
ASHGABAT
BISHKEK
DUSHANBE
KABUL
ISLAMABAD
NEW DELHI
KATHMANDU
THIMPH
Agra
Indus
MUSCAT
Ganges
Brahm
Arabian Sea
GIR FOREST NATIONAL PARK
Tropic of Cancer
DACCA
Bay of Bengal
Western Ghats
RA
Palk Strait
Sri Lanka
COLOMBO
Maldives
MALE
S
W

IN FOCUS

INDIAN RHINOCEROS This rhino spends much of its day in water to keep cool. It comes ashore in the evening or early morning to gather leaves and grass with the help of its flexible upper lip. Its single horn can be 20 inches (50 cm) long.

This young rhino's horn is not yet fully grown

Wallowing in water

Striped hyena
Carrion is the main source of food for this animal, but it does also kill its own prey. Its teeth and jaws are so strong that it can even crush bones, teeth, and horns.

Snake killer
Surprisingly, the mongoose can beat a cobra in a fight. It moves fast, making it hard for the cobra to strike on target. The mongoose darts in and seizes the snake at the back of its head to deliver a killing bite.

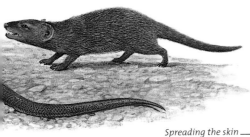

Spotted deer
These shy, nervous animals are the most common deer in India. They often gather under trees where monkeys are feeding and eat up any fruits they drop. They are a favorite prey of tigers.

Spreading the skin at the sides of its head makes the cobra look more threatening

King cobra
The king cobra is the longest of all venomous snakes. Most are about 10 feet (3 m) long, but some grow to 16½ feet (5 m). Other snakes are its main prey, but it can kill an elephant.

Nilgai
This member of the cattle family lives in groups of up to 20. Only males have horns. When they battle for territory, they drop to their knees before lunging with their horns.

IN DANGER! Loss of habitat and poaching for body parts have reduced the number of sloth bears. They live in forests and feed mostly on termites and ants. Sloth bears open their nest with their strong claws, then noisily suck out the insects.

The Lower Mekong

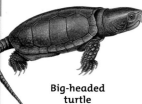

Big-headed turtle

THE MEKONG RIVER is at the heart of this region. The river starts farther north and winds its way through the forests of Laos, Myanmar (Burma), Cambodia, and Thailand before ending in the Mekong delta in Vietnam. As well as forests, this region has vast swamps, mangroves, and grasslands that are flooded at some times of the year. It is home to a huge variety of birds, as well as deer, turtles, and other creatures. New species are still being discovered here—about 145 in the Greater Mekong area in 2009.

Map labels: THIMPHU, DACCA, Bay of Bengal, HANOI, VIENTIANE, RANGOON, BANGKOK, PHNOM PENH, Mekong, INDIAN OCEAN, Andaman Islands, Andaman Sea, Gulf of Thailand, KUALA LUMPUR, SINGAPORE

Mekong landscape

The Mekong is 2,703 miles (4,350 km) long and is the longest river in Southeast Asia. More than 240 different kinds of fish live in its waters, many of them found nowhere else.

Siamese crocodile

The Lower Mekong is one of the few places where this crocodile is still seen in the wild. It is one of the world's rarest reptiles.

Jaws are studded with up to 66 teeth

Irrawaddy dolphin

Siamese giant carp

IN FOCUS

EXPERT CLIMBER The clouded leopard leaps through the trees with ease as it hunts monkeys and birds. Its legs are short but strong, and its long tail helps it balance as it climbs. It hunts mostly at night and has excellent eyesight.

This leopard has the largest canine teeth for its skull size of any cat.

A male is about 3 feet (90 cm) long with a tail of the same length. Females are smaller.

Fingerlike toes with short claws

Red-shanked douc monkey

This monkey, with its chestnut-red legs, is one of the most colorful of all mammals. It lives in the treetops in tropical forests, feeding on leaves and some fruits.

Upside-down parrot

The blue-crowned hanging parrot gets its name from its habit of hanging upside down to roost, as well as from its blue head feathers. The female has a smaller blue crown than the male.

Short-clawed otter

Most otters catch prey in their mouths, but this animal finds and grabs fish, crabs, and mollusks with its sensitive, partially webbed front feet. It is the smallest of the otters.

Life in the river

Birds, cats, and other hunters come to the river to find turtles, fish, and other prey. One of the largest fish is the giant carp, which is the biggest of its family and can weigh up to 660 pounds (300 kg).

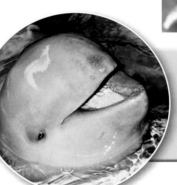

IN DANGER! The Irrawaddy dolphin, which lives in the Mekong as well as in coastal waters, is on the brink of extinction. The river population is particularly endangered.

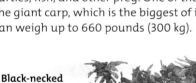

White-throated kingfisher

Black-necked crane

Siamese crocodile

Giant ibis

Smooth-coated otter

Mekong wagtail

Giant Asian pond turtle

Spiny-breasted giant frog

Fishing cat

Mountains of Southwest China

Hog badger

HOME TO GIANT PANDAS, these mountains stretch around 100,400 square miles (260,000 km²). The dense forests cloaking their slopes have the greatest variety of plants of any temperate forests in the world: there are at least 12,000 plant species—about a third of which are found nowhere else. There are also more than 200 kinds of mammals and 600 bird species, but many of these are becoming increasingly rare as large areas of forest are logged and cleared for farmland.

Mountain forests
More than 40 areas of forest in this region have been set aside as reserves where giant pandas can live in safety.

Noisy mountain bird
The speckled laughing thrush is found only in these mountains and is now rare. Its name comes from its noisy cackling call. Fruits and insects are its main food.

Red goral
Nimble-footed goral belong to the goat and sheep family. They live in woodlands high up on mountain slopes and are expert climbers and jumpers. They feed mostly on lichen.

White-eared pheasant
This pheasant uses its strong beak to dig up roots and bulbs, but it also feeds on seeds, leaves, and insects. Male and females look alike, but females are slightly smaller.

Male and female takin have horns up to 12 inches (30 cm) long

Takin
The plump golden-haired takin is a goat-antelope, which lives in high bamboo forests. Takins live in groups and feed on almost any plant they can find.

IN DANGER! The red panda lives in these mountains and the Himalayas and feeds almost entirely on bamboo leaves. Its numbers are decreasing because of habitat loss and hunting.

Golden monkey
This beautiful monkey lives only in China. It spends most of its time in the trees, feeding on leaves and flowers, and is more often heard than seen. There are probably only about 10,000 left in the wild.

▶▶ FIT FOR LIFE

BAMBOO EATERS Giant pandas live only in this area and have suffered greatly from loss of habitat as the forests have shrunk. They feed on bamboo, and because their food is not very nourishing, they must spend nearly all their waking hours eating. There are now only about 1,600 giant pandas left in the wild.

Pandas have short blunt claws on their front feet.

Pandas walk on the toes of their hind feet.

An enlarged wrist bone on each front paw acts like a thumb to help the panda handle bamboo shoots.

A panda eats about 40 pounds (18 kg) of bamboo a day.

Rainforests of Southeast Asia

Atlas beetle

TROPICAL RAINFORESTS can thrive in much of Southeast Asia, where the climate is generally warm and wet all year long. These great forests were once thought to have the largest range of plant and animal species of any jungle area, but sadly huge areas have already been lost and the logging continues. Many of the forests' extraordinary inhabitants, such as orangutans and proboscis monkeys, are also becoming dangerously rare; conservationists are working on protecting areas of forest as reserves.

Giant moth

The Atlas moth has the largest wing area of any moth. Adult moths live for only two weeks and do not feed, but as caterpillars they ate lots of jungle plants.

Wings measure 10 to 12 inches (25 to 30 cm) across

Towering trees
Forests on the island of Borneo are dominated by huge trees called dipterocarps. They can grow to more than 145 feet (45 m) high.

▶▶ FIT FOR LIFE

GLIDING Trees in these forests are tall, and it can take a long time to get down to the ground to move to a neighboring tree. Instead, a range of creatures manage to glide from branch to branch with amazing skill. Being able to travel through the trees in this way is also useful when hunting or escaping from predators.

A flying frog stretches out its toe webbing and the flaps at the side of its body to act as a kind of parachute to help it glide.

Flying snake

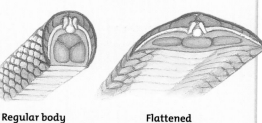

Regular body shape

Flattened for flying

As a flying snake launches itself into the air, it flattens its body to about twice its usual width. It can then glide gently through the air and land on another branch.

Slow loris
This little primate is slow but still a very good climber with a powerful grip. It eats birds' eggs and preys on insects and other small creatures.

IN FOCUS

FOREST APES Orangutans are the only great apes found outside Africa. These forest dwellers look after their young for longer than any primate other than humans. There is a lot to teach them, such as what to eat and how to find it, as well as how to build a sleeping nest and shelter from the rain.

An orangutan's hand is much like ours, with four long fingers and an opposable thumb.

Mother and young

Golden-capped fruit bat
This is one of the largest, heaviest bats in the world—a male can weigh nearly 2½ pounds (1.1 kg). During the day, the bat roosts in the trees; it flies out at night to feed on fruits.

Wings measure up to 5½ feet (1.7 m) across

Figs are this bat's favorite food

Nesting hornbills
The hornbill nests in a tree hole, and her mate helps her wall up part of the entrance with mud to keep her and the eggs safe. He passes food to her through a small hole.

Tarsier
One of the smallest of all primates, the tarsier is about the size of a human fist. It lives alone and sleeps in the trees during the day. At night, it preys on insects and lizards.

Praying mantis
The color and shape of this mantis are an almost perfect match for the orchid flowers it lives among. Insects visit the flowers and get snapped up by the mantis.

Spiky front legs for grasping prey

IN DANGER! The proboscis monkey lives only in Borneo and is now at serious risk of extinction. There are probably only about 3,000 left in the wild. Large parts of its forest home have been destroyed, and this slow-moving monkey is also easy to hunt.

Australasia

DESERT AND SEMIDESERT cover more than two-thirds of Australia, but it is still home to more kinds of animals than Europe and North America put together. Nearly all of these, and the creatures on neighboring New Guinea and New Zealand, are unique and found nowhere else in the world. Most marsupials—mammals with pouches, such as the kangaroo—live in Australia and New Guinea, and the only egg-laying mammals—the echidna and the platypus—are found here too. There are flightless birds, such as the emu and kiwi, and many kinds of colorful parrots and birds-of-paradise.

Boxing kangaroos

Male kangaroos fight one another over leadership of a herd or when competing for females in the breeding season. They can do serious damage with the long, sharp claws on their back feet.

IN FOCUS

PARROT BEAKS Most parrots have curved beaks, but these differ in shape according to their diet. The palm cockatoo and the gang-gang have strong beaks for breaking open hard seed cases and unripe fruits, while the corella uses its slender beak to take seeds from cones. The fig parrot uses its tongue, not its beak, to collect nectar from flowers.

| Palm cockatoo | Gang-gang cockatoo | Corella parrot | Double-eyed fig parrot |

Equator

Jazirah Doberai

Ja

Pegunungan Maoke

Birdwing butterfly
see page 96

Pulau Dolak

N
Gu

Torres

Cape Yo

Arafura Sea

Melville Island
Bathurst Island

Cassowary
see page 98

Darwin○

Arnhem Land

○Katherine

Timor Sea

Gulf of Carpentaria

Wyndham ○

Barkly Tableland

Kimberley

○ Derby

Tennant Creek ○

○ Mount I

○Broome

A U S T R A L I

Port Hedland ○

Great Sandy Desert

Barrow Island ○

○ Alice Springs

Pilbara

Emu
see page 101

Simpson Desert

Great Arte Basin

North West Cape

Gibson Desert

○Carnarvon

Koala
see page 102

Lake Eyre

Great Victoria Desert

Platypus
see page 103

Lake Torrens

Flinders Ranges

Geraldton○

Lake Gairdner

Broke

○ Kalgoorlie

Ceduna ○

Nullarbor Plain

Adelaide ○

Great Australian Bight

Kangaroo Island

Perth ○

Esperance ○

A warning to drivers to watch out for wombats

Mo
Gan

Cape Leeuwin

○ Albany

S O U T H E R N

Scale

0 ———————— 400 miles

0 ———————— 400 kilometers

O C E A

NEXT 12 km

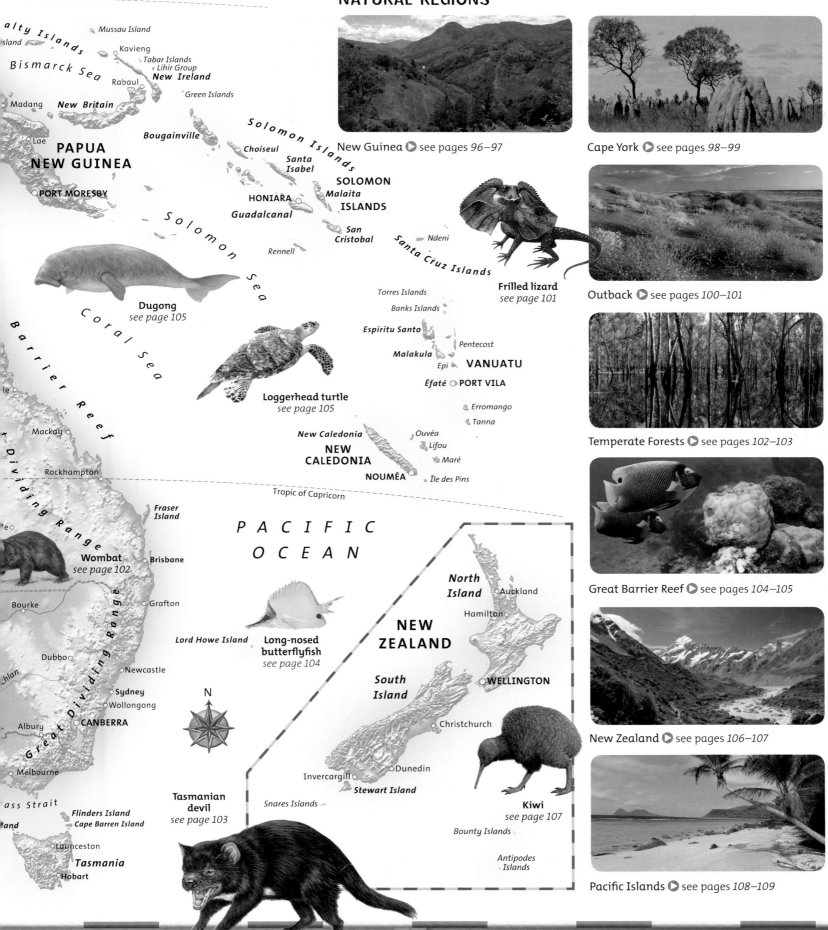

NATURAL REGIONS

New Guinea ▶ see pages 96–97

Cape York ▶ see pages 98–99

Outback ▶ see pages 100–101

Temperate Forests ▶ see pages 102–103

Great Barrier Reef ▶ see pages 104–105

New Zealand ▶ see pages 106–107

Pacific Islands ▶ see pages 108–109

Frilled lizard
see page 101

Dugong
see page 105

Loggerhead turtle
see page 105

Wombat
see page 102

Long-nosed
butterflyfish
see page 104

Tasmanian
devil
see page 103

Kiwi
see page 107

PAPUA
NEW GUINEA

PORT MORESBY

Bismarck Sea

Mussau Island

Kavieng

Tabar Islands
Lihir Group

New Ireland

Rabaul

Green Islands

Madang

New Britain

Lae

Bougainville

Choiseul

Santa
Isabel

SOLOMON

HONIARA

Malaita

ISLANDS

Guadalcanal

San
Cristobal

Rennell

Ndeni

Santa Cruz Islands

Torres Islands

Banks Islands

Espíritu Santo

Malakula

Pentecost

Epi

VANUATU

Éfaté ◌ PORT VILA

Erromango

Tanna

New Caledonia

NEW
CALEDONIA

NOUMÉA

Ouvéa

Lifou

Maré

Île des Pins

Coral Sea

Solomon Sea

Solomon Islands

Barrier Reef

Mackay

Rockhampton

Tropic of Capricorn

PACIFIC
OCEAN

Fraser
Island

Brisbane

Grafton

Lord Howe Island

NEW
ZEALAND

North
Island

Auckland

Hamilton

Great Dividing Range

Bourke

Dubbo

Newcastle

Sydney

Wollongong

Albury ◌ CANBERRA

Melbourne

South
Island

WELLINGTON

Christchurch

N

Invercargill

Dunedin

Snares Islands

Stewart Island

Bounty Islands

Antipodes
Islands

ass Strait

Flinders Island
Cape Barren Island

Launceston

Tasmania

Hobart

New Guinea

Swallowtail butterfly

THIS IS THE SECOND-LARGEST ISLAND in the world. It features rich and varied landscapes, including a long mountain chain that runs down the center of the island, coastal mangrove swamps, and a huge tropical rainforest. The island is home to some amazing creatures, two-thirds of which are found only there, and many spectacular plants, including more kinds of orchids than anywhere else. The climate is hot all year long, and there is plenty of rain, mostly falling from December through March.

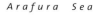

Biak

Vogelkop Peninsula

Jayapura

Pegunungan Maoke

Sepik

Central

New Guin

Kepulauan Aru

Mc

Fly

Arafura Sea

Torres Str

Tropical forest
New Guinea's tropical rainforest is the third largest in the world and covers an area about the size of Spain. Huge efforts are being made to protect this unique forest.

Goodfellow's tree kangaroo
New Guinea's kangaroos are somewhat different from those in Australia—they climb trees and spend most of their time high above the ground.

Birdwing butterfly
Birdwings are some of the largest of all butterflies, with wings up to 12 inches (30 cm) across. This Poseidon birdwing lives in the lower levels of the New Guinea rainforest.

Fierce lizard
The mangrove monitor grows up to 4 feet (1.2 m) long. It spends much of its time in water but also climbs trees in search of insects, birds, and lizards.

Spotted cuscus
This common marsupial is a member of one of the possum families. It feeds on leaves, fruits, and flowers, and it has traditionally been cooked and eaten by local people.

Manus Island

Bismarck Archipelago

New Ireland

Bismarck Sea

Rabaul

Madang

New Britain

Huon Peninsula

Solomon Sea

Kokoda

D'Entrecasteaux Islands

PORT MORESBY

Owen Stanley Ra.

Pig-nosed turtle
Its long snout acts like a snorkel to allow this turtle to breathe while underwater. The snout is also very sensitive and helps the turtle find food.

Skillful climber
The green tree python waits coiled around a branch, ready to strike at passing prey such as rodents and birds. It grows to more than 7 feet (2.1 m) long.

IN DANGER! The long-beaked echidna is one of the very few monotreme mammals—these lay eggs instead of giving birth. It uses its long snout to dig in the ground for worms, then sucks them up. This animal is now rare.

Pritchard's snake-necked turtle
This long-necked turtle lives only in New Guinea. It's now rare because so many have been caught illegally for the pet trade.

Victoria crowned pigeon
The largest living pigeon, this bird lives only in New Guinea rainforests, where it feeds on fruits, seeds, and snails.

IN FOCUS

BIRDS-OF-PARADISE Most of these amazing birds live in New Guinea. The males have very ornate and colorful feathers, which they use to show off to the much plainer females in complex mating dances and displays.

Raggiana bird-of-paradise

Superb bird-of-paradise

Huon astrapia

Blue bird-of-paradise

Cape York

Striped opossum

THE NORTHERNMOST POINT of Australia is Cape York—a large, mostly flat peninsula. Although some of this remote land has been cleared for agriculture, there is still plenty of unspoiled wilderness, with forests, woodlands, coastal wetlands, and mangrove swamps. Most important is the area of tropical rainforest, where there is an incredible range of plants and wildlife. Some of the animals here are also found in New Guinea—a reminder that the two landmasses were once joined.

N

Torres Strait
Thursday Island
Cape York

Great Barrier

Coral Sea

Cape Grenville

Weipa
Cape
Lockhart River

York
Coen

Gulf of Carpentaria

Cape Melville

Peninsula
Holroyd

Cape Flattery

Kowanyama
Palmer

Cooktown

Reef

Mitchell

Mornington Island

Cairns

Normanton

Innisfail

Agile wallaby

This wallaby is the most common kangaroo in this area. It lives in coastal regions and wetlands and is a good swimmer. It generally feeds at night on leaves and grass.

Saltwater crocodile

This fierce hunter is the world's biggest crocodile. It can grow up to 23 feet (7 m) long, although most are smaller. It is at home in the sea and estuaries as well as rivers.

IN DANGER! The cassowary is a flightless bird that feeds mostly on fruits. Its numbers are falling because of habitat loss and hunting, and many have also been killed by dogs.

Brush turkey

Orange-thighed tree frog

Eastern gray kangaroo

The eastern gray kangaroo lives in forest and grassland. The joey stays in its mother's pouch for at least eight months before it ventures out.

Sulfur-crested cockatoo

Noisy flocks of these birds feed on seeds on the ground but fly up into the trees to roost. They are popular pets.

S

Spectacled flying fox

During the day, this bat rests hanging upside down from a tree branch, with its wings wrapped around it. At dusk, it flies off to feed on fruits, as well as flower nectar and pollen.

IN FOCUS

MANGROVE FORESTS Mangrove trees grow along the coasts of Cape York. They are adapted to withstand being swamped by seawater at high tide and have long roots that absorb oxygen from the air. The mangroves are home to many kinds of crabs, fish, and birds.

The archer fish spits out a jet of water to knock insects off leaves overhanging the water, then snaps them up.

Striated heron

Gobies

Archer fish

Stilt roots

Fiddler crabs

Rainforest floor

The forest floor may look bare, but lots of insects and other small creatures live there. Lizards, snakes, and frogs find shelter and plentiful prey, while many birds come to gobble up seeds, fallen fruits, and other foods.

Chameleon gecko

Scrub python

Giant forest cricket

Centipede

Outback

Thorny devil

A HUGE PART OF THE INTERIOR of Australia is covered by very dry land—the outback. But this is not all parched desert—there are vast areas of rough grassland and low woodland, as well as some of the biggest sand dunes in the world. Despite the lack of water, the outback is full of life. Millions of termites and ants feed on the spinifex grass and its seeds, and they in turn are food for countless lizards as well as birds and small mammals. Some creatures manage without drinking at all. Others shelter from the daytime heat in burrows.

N

Timor Sea
Darwin
Arnhem Land
Gulf of Carpentaria
Coral Sea
Cairns
Kimberley
Broome
Tanami Desert
Great Sandy Desert
Pilbara
Alice Springs
MacDonnell Ranges
Carnarvon
Gibson Desert
Simpson Desert
Great Victoria Desert
Great Dividing Range
Brisbane
Nullarbor Plain
Kalgoorlie
Darling
Perth
Great Australian Bight
Adelaide
Murray
CANBERRA
Sydney
Melbourne
Hobart
W
S

Outback scenery
At the heart of the outback is the area now designated as the Uluru–Kata Tjuta National Park, where famed sandstone rock formations rise from the dry, flat plains.

Sand goanna

Tussocks spinifex

Night creature
The bilby is a small marsupial with long ears like a rabbit. It shelters from the heat in a burrow during the day and comes out at night to feed on anything it can find, from insects to seeds and fruits.

Bearded dragon

IN DANGER! The kowari is now rare because of habitat loss. It does not have to drink and gets all the water it needs from its food. Insects, lizards, and small birds are its main prey.

White-winged fairy wren

Wild dogs

In packs or alone, the dingo roams the outback hunting small animals such as rodents, lizards, and birds. Dingoes may be descended from wild dogs, possibly brought from Asia by sailors more than 4,000 years ago.

Wedge-tailed eagle

This sharp-eyed eagle is the largest bird of prey in Australia. It soars high above the ground, searching for prey such as rabbits, then swoops on its victim at high speed. It kills prey with its strong talons.

Frilled lizard

If in danger, this lizard warns off its enemies by erecting the skin around its neck to make itself seem larger and by hissing loudly.

Emu chicks

Watchful parent

The male emu not only incubates his partner's eggs but also looks after the chicks once they hatch. The flightless emu is the biggest bird in Australia.

Mulgara

👁 IN FOCUS

SURVIVAL STRATEGY Frogs need to keep their skin moist, so life in the outback is hard. In times of drought, the water-holding frog manages to survive by burrowing underground and making a cocoon of shed skin around itself to retain moisture.

Spinifex grasslands

Tough, spiky spinifex grass grows over large areas of the outback. Only termites can actually eat the grass, but other creatures come to it for shelter, to eat its seeds, and to prey on one another.

Sand-swimming skink

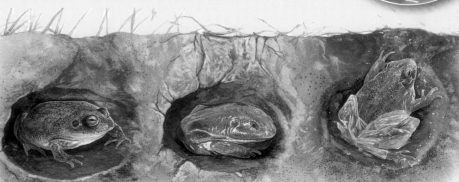

The frog digs a burrow underground where it can hide in safety while it waits for rain.

Once the cocoon is made, the frog slows its body down to use as little energy as possible.

When the rains come, the frog sheds its cocoon and digs its way to the surface to feed and mate.

Temperate Forests

Quoll

ENOUGH RAIN FALLS in South and Southeast Australia for forests and woodlands to thrive. Eucalyptus trees are the most important plants, and there are hundreds of different kinds, including the mighty swamp gum or mountain ash. One of the tallest trees in the world, this eucalyptus grows to 300 feet (90 m) high. When they flower, eucalyptus trees attract hordes of nectar feeders such as possums and fruit bats, as well as many kinds of birds that pollinate the trees as they feast on the nectar.

Forest fires
Some forests in this area depend on fires to stimulate new growth. The seeds cannot start to grow until a forest fire burns off old plants and at the same time activates the new seeds.

The numbat's tongue can be half the length of its body

Leaf eater
The koala is a marsupial, not a bear. A slow-moving creature, it lives in trees and eats eucalyptus leaves. It gets moisture from its food and rarely needs to drink.

Wombat
The strong-clawed wombat digs a burrow to shelter in during the day. At night, this marsupial comes out to feed on grass, roots, and bark.

▶▶▶ **FIT FOR LIFE**

RARE POSSUM The mountain pygmy possum was thought to be extinct, but it was found living high on mountains in this area. It survives the harsh climate by building up its reserves of body fat in the summer, then hibernating during the cold, wet winter months.

In the winter, this little creature hibernates in a tunnel under the snow and lives off its fat reserves.

In the summer, the possum feeds on the plentiful bogong moths and gets as fat as it can.

IN DANGER! Now found only in Tasmania, the fierce Tasmanian devil is in danger of extinction because of a serious infectious cancer, which has killed thousands of animals.

Greater glider

Australian marsupials
Many of Australia's 140 or so kinds of marsupials live in these forests and have adapted to different lifestyles. Gliders and possums clamber in the trees, feeding on leaves, sap, and insects, while the quoll hunts small creatures on the ground.

Sugar glider

Ringtail possum

Numbat
Termites are the main food of this small marsupial. It digs in the ground with its pointed snout, then laps up its insect prey with its long, sticky tongue.

Rock wallaby

Underwater hunter
The platypus hunts insects, worms, and other river creatures with the help of its sensitive beak. The male has a venomous spur on each back foot.

Southern brown bandicoot

Spotted-tailed quoll

Marsupial mole

Satin bowerbird
The male bowerbird attracts a mate by making a bower of sticks on the ground, which he decorates with colorful, usually blue, objects. A separate nest for the eggs is made later.

Great Barrier Reef

Meyers butterflyfish

THE WORLD'S BIGGEST CORAL REEF, the Great Barrier Reef stretches about 1,430 miles (2,300 km) along the Australian coastline and covers an area larger than Italy. It is one of the world's great natural wonders. As well as the corals themselves, more than 1,500 kinds of fish live on the reef and countless other creatures, such as crabs, starfish, mollusks, and sponges, make their home among the nooks and crannies. Much larger animals, including whales, sharks, and turtles, regularly visit the reef to find food.

N

Cape York

FAR NORTHERN
MANAGEMENT AREA

Coral

Sea

Great

Lizard Island

P A C I F I C

Cooktown

CAIRNS/COOKTOWN
MANAGEMENT AREA

O C E A N

Cairns

Barrier

GREAT BARRIER REEF

MARINE PARK

TOWNSVILLE/WHITSUNDAY
MANAGEMENT AREA

Townsville

Whitsunday Island

Reef

Mackay

MACKAY/CAPRICORN
MANAGEMENT
AREA

Rockhampton

Heron Island

Protecting the reef
Pollution, overfishing, and global warming all cause damage to the delicate reef system. Part of the reef is now a protected marine park, containing marine sanctuaries.

Marine life
Coral reefs are made up of the rocky skeletons of tiny coral animals and are some of the busiest of all wildlife areas. There are more than 350 kinds of corals living on the Great Barrier Reef.

Filter feeder
The southern minke whale is a baleen whale. This means that it feeds by using the fringed plates in its mouth to filter small creatures from the water.

W

Moorish idol

Brain coral

Long-nosed butterflyfish

Elkhorn coral

Blue surgeonfish

S

Dugong

This large, sea-living mammal feeds on sea grasses. When the dugong dives, it can stay underwater without breathing for up to 15 minutes.

WEEDY SEA DRAGONS These fish are relatives of the sea horse and live around weed beds and reefs just to the south of the Great Barrier Reef. Their strange shape and leafy fins make them hard to spot as they swim among waving fronds of weed. They can grow up to 18 inches (46 cm) long.

Manta ray

The manta is one of the largest of all fish and grows up to 23 feet (7 m) across. It moves gracefully through the ocean by beating its fins up and down, like wings.

Christmas tree worms

These worms use their spiral-shaped tentacles for taking tiny animals and other food from the water and for breathing.

Predatory turtle

The huge loggerhead catches jellyfish, crabs, and fish but also feeds on seaweed. Like all turtles, it is now very rare.

Parrotfish

Giant clam

Staghorn coral

Table coral

Crown-of-thorns starfish

Clown anemonefish

Orangespine unicornfish

New Zealand

Hochstetter's frog

THE TWO MAIN ISLANDS that make up New Zealand feature spectacular mountain ranges, fiords, glaciers, and temperate rainforests. Its isolation has led to New Zealand being populated by a range of extraordinary creatures, including many flightless birds. There are no native, ground-living mammals—birds have taken their place—but some have been introduced by humans. These animals, such as stoats, cats, and rats, have caused some of New Zealand's unique wildlife to become perilously rare.

N

Cape Reinga

Auckland

North Island

Bay of Plenty

East Cape

T a s m a n

Taupo

Hawke Bay

S e a

Hastings

Cape Farewell

Cook Strait

WELLINGTON

Cape Palliser

South Island

PACIFIC

Southern Alps

Christchurch

Banks Peninsula

Canterbury Bight

OCEAN

Queenstown

Otago Peninsula
Dunedin

Invercargill

Stewart Island

W

Rugged shores

New Zealand has a very long coastline—more than 9,300 miles (15,000 km). Much of it is wild and rugged and indented with fiords, coves, and bays.

New Zealand sea lion

This rare sea lion lives in New Zealand waters and breeds on small islands off the coast of the South Island. Males are twice the size of females.

IN FOCUS

NIGHT PARROT The kakapo is not only the world's only flightless parrot, it is also the heaviest and the only one that is active at night. Now extremely rare, it lives on a couple of small offshore islands and is carefully protected by conservation workers.

Roots, seeds, fruits, and other plant food are the main diet of the kakapo.

Endangered dolphin

Hector's dolphin is one of the rarest in the world and lives only in the seas off New Zealand. There are probably about 8,000 left in the wild.

S

▶▶ FIT FOR LIFE

GROUND BIRD The kiwi cannot fly and finds all its food on the forest floor. It has nostrils at the end of its beak and uses its sense of smell to root out insects and worms. It lays large eggs—up to a quarter the size of the female. The egg of a brown kiwi is as big as a man's hand.

Tuatara
This creature might look like a lizard but belongs to a group all of its own, which dates back to before the dinosaurs. It eats insects.

Mountain parrot
The kea lives above the forest line in the Southern Alps of New Zealand. An intelligent and playful bird, it feeds on plants, insects, and anything else it can find.

Heaviest insect
The giant weta, a kind of cricket, is the world's heaviest insect and weighs up to 2½ ounces (70 g). It scurries around the forest floor, feeding on plants.

Yellow-eyed penguin
This penguin stands 25½ inches (65 cm) tall and is the fourth-largest penguin in the world. It nests in forests, often near a tree or log.

Hamilton's frog
There are only four types of frogs native to New Zealand, and all are now rare. This frog shelters among mossy rocks during the day and comes out at night to find insects to eat.

Pacific Islands

Giant land snail

FAR FROM ANY OTHER LAND, these islands in the southwest Pacific have many plants and animals that are found nowhere else. Lord Howe Island and Norfolk Island are both volcanic, and subtropical rainforest is the main vegetation. Around 75 percent of Lord Howe Island is now a Natural World Heritage Site, and there are efforts to rid the island of introduced species such as rats and goats that have destroyed some native life. New Caledonia is home to a particularly wide range of unique plants, reptiles, and birds, including the kagu.

N

Coral Sea

New Caledonia

NOUMEA

Brisbane

PACIFIC OCEAN

Norfolk Island

Port Macquarie

↘ *Lord Howe Island*

Sydney

Tasman Sea

Kagu
Despite its large wings, this bird is flightless. It feeds mostly on worms, snakes, and lizards and has a strange barking call.

W

Rare seabird
Murphy's petrel flies over the Pacific and breeds on a number of islands. It nests in shallow scrapes on the ground and lays a single egg.

Ornate flying fox
This fruit bat lives only on the islands of New Caledonia. It feeds mostly on fruits, squeezing out the juice in its mouth and spitting out the pulp and seeds.

Black rat
The black rat was introduced accidentally to these islands and has caused huge problems since it preys on native animals.

IN DANGER! The Lord Howe woodhen was once common on Lord Howe Island. Sadly, it was hunted for food and killed by cats and pigs introduced to the island until there were only about 30 birds left. It is now protected, and numbers have risen to about 200.

S

Purple swamphen

This wading bird lives on islands all over the Pacific. It makes its nest in reedbeds and feeds on plants as well as fish, insects, and worms.

Sooty terns

Large colonies of sooty terns nest on Lord Howe Island and other islands. Each pair lays a single egg, and both parents help incubate the egg and feed the chick.

IN FOCUS

PROVIDENCE PETRELS These seabirds are seen across the western Pacific, where they dive for food such as fish and squid. They breed only on Lord Howe Island and Phillip Island, a small island off Norfolk Island. Each pair lays just one egg in a chamber at the end of a burrow or in a rock crevice.

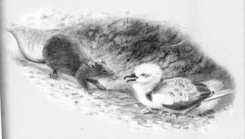

Parents take turns to incubate their egg in their grass-lined, underground nest.

Providence petrel in flight

The young chick is left alone when its parents go to feed, so it is in danger from predators such as rats.

Giant stick insect

The Lord Howe phasmid grows to 5 inches (13 cm) long. It was thought to be extinct, but a small number survive, and more are being bred.

N

Poles and Oceans

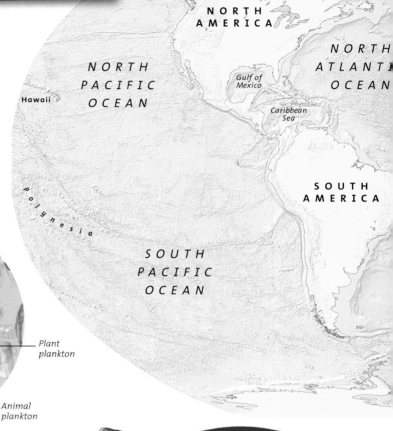

Gray-headed albatross

ABOUT TWO-THIRDS of our planet is covered by oceans. There has been life in the sea for far longer than on land, but still we know less about these ocean worlds, and the extraordinary creatures that live here, than we do about the rest of life on Earth. All of the five oceans flow into one another—there can be no borders in the sea—but the different areas have their own names. The climate of the Arctic and Antarctic at the North and South Poles is so cold that large areas of sea freeze over during the winter months.

Beaufort Sea

Baffin Bay

Hudson Bay

Labrador Sea

Gulf of Alaska

NORTH AMERICA

NORTH ATLANTIC OCEAN

NORTH PACIFIC OCEAN

Gulf of Mexico

Hawaii

Caribbean Sea

Polynesia

SOUTH AMERICA

SOUTH PACIFIC OCEAN

Plant plankton

Animal plankton

NATURAL REGIONS

The Arctic ▶ see pages *112–113*

Antarctica ▶ see pages *114–115*

Atlantic Ocean ▶ see pages *118–119*

Plankton
Tiny floating plant and animal plankton are the basis of all life in the ocean. Animal plankton eat plant plankton and then in turn are eaten by larger creatures.

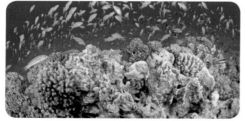

Indian Ocean ▶ see pages *116–117*

Pacific Ocean ▶ see pages *120–121*

Great white shark
The great white is the largest of all predatory fish and one of the fiercest hunters in the ocean. It can grow up to 20 feet (6 m) long.

W

S

Map labels

ARCTIC OCEAN

North Sea

EUROPE

Black Sea

Mediterranean Sea

AFRICA

Red Sea

Arabian Sea

ASIA

Sea of Okhotsk

Bering Sea

Sea of Japan

Yellow Sea

East China Sea

NORTH PACIFIC OCEAN

Philippine Sea

South China Sea

Micronesia

Bay of Bengal

INDIAN OCEAN

AUSTRALIA

Coral Sea

Great Australian Bight

Tasman Sea

SOUTHERN OCEAN

ANTARCTICA

SOUTH ATLANTIC OCEAN

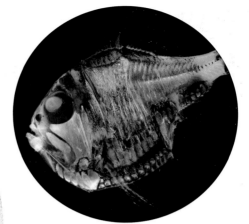

Deep-sea fish

The hatchetfish lives in the dark ocean depths. It feeds on plankton and other small creatures, which it finds with the help of the light-producing organs on the underside of its body.

Ocean zones

Just as on land, life in the ocean depends on plants. Plant plankton can only live in the sunlit surface layer, so this is where most sea creatures live. Below this, there is little or no light, and life is increasingly sparse.

Sunlight zone
Plant plankton can live here in the top 660 feet (200 m).

Twilight zone
Below 660 feet (200 m), there is not enough light for plants.

Midnight zone
Below 3,300 feet (1,000 m), there is no light, except from luminous animals.

Low tide

High tide

Continental shelf

Continental slope

Continental rise

Seabed

ATLAS OF ANIMALS

The Arctic

THIS ICY LAND LIES AT THE FAR NORTH of the world. Within the Arctic Circle, which is at a latitude of about 66°N, are the northern parts of North America, Greenland, Europe, and Asia, and the Arctic Ocean. Much of the Arctic Ocean is covered by sea ice. This is at its greatest extent during the winter and shrinks back in the summer, but there is always ice at its center. Surrounding the ocean are the tundra regions. This land is blanketed by snow in the winter, but in the spring the snow thaws and low-growing plants flourish. Many insects and other creatures come to the tundra to find food during the brief summer.

Arctic tern

Harsh landscape
Ice floes—floating chunks of ice—make a handy place for walrus to rest. They haul themselves out of the water with their tusks.

▶▶▶ FIT FOR LIFE

COLOR CHANGE In the summer, when the snows melt on the tundra, the Arctic fox has a brownish coat that helps it hide among the rocks and low plants. In the winter, its coat turns snowy white, again helping it stay out of sight as it stalks prey.

Arctic fox and cubs **Fox jumping on prey**

Beluga whales
These chubby whales live in Arctic waters all year long and have a thick layer of fatty blubber to keep them warm. They are among the noisiest whales and make a range of different squeaks, chirps, whistles, and clicks.

IN DANGER! Little is known about the narwhal, but this whale's numbers are threatened by climate change and hunting. The male narwhal's spiral tusk is actually an overgrown tooth and can be up to 8 feet (2.4 m) long.

IN FOCUS

TOP PREDATORS Polar bears are the largest of all land-living carnivores. Their thick, waterproof fur helps protect them both in and out of water, as they hunt seals and other prey.

In the fall, the female polar bear digs a den under the snow, where she gives birth to her cubs.

Airhole

Main entrance

Bears watch at breathing holes in the ice, ready to catch seals.

Bearded seal
Long whiskers give this seal its name. It lives in shallow Arctic waters and feeds mostly on bottom-living creatures, such as clams, crabs, and worms.

Musk oxen
Mighty musk oxen are perfectly adapted to Arctic weather. They have a double-layered coat that keeps them warm, even in temperatures of −58°F (−50°C). The oxen huddle together if attacked.

Arctic shark
The Greenland shark is the only shark that lives in Arctic waters. It generally stays in deep water, below 660 feet (200 m), and hunts fish and seals.

Flying pirates
Parasitic jaegers, also known as Arctic skuas, chase other birds and steal their catches. In the breeding season, each pair rears two chicks in a nest on the ground.

Sea spider

Antarctica

THE DRIEST, WINDIEST place on Earth, Antarctica is also one of the coldest. In fact, the lowest temperature ever recorded was at a research station here—an astonishing −128.56°F (−89.2°C). Even in the summer the temperatures stay below freezing. Antarctica is the fifth-largest continent, and much of it is covered by a huge ice sheet, which contains as much as 90 percent of all the freshwater on Earth. The continent is surrounded by the Southern Ocean.

South Georgia

South Sandwich Islands

SOUTHERN

Scotia Sea

South Orkney Islands

Antarctic Circle

Fimbul Ice Shelf

Riis

Falkland Islands

South Shetland Islands

Riiser-Larsen Ice Shelf

Tierra del Fuego

Drake Passage

Bransfield Strait

Brunt Ice Shelf

Queen

Larsen Ice Shelf

Weddell Sea

Filchner Ice Shelf

Alexander Island

Antarctic Peninsula

Berkner Island

Ronne Ice Shelf

ANTA

Bellingshausen Sea

West Antarctica

△ South P

Peter I Island

Marie Byrd Land

Horlick Mtns

Transantarcti

Amundsen Sea

Ross Ice Shelf

Getz Ice Shelf

Ross Sea

McMur Soun

Cape Adare

Antarctic Circle

SOU

Taking the plunge

At only 30 inches (76 cm) tall, Adélie penguins are the smallest Antarctic penguins. Here, a group dives off an iceberg to hunt for food such as krill.

Largest wingspan

The wandering albatross has wings that measure up to 11½ feet (3.5 m) from tip to tip—the largest of any bird. This bird spends most of its life soaring over the ocean and only comes to land in the breeding season.

Chinstrap penguins

These are the most common penguins in Antarctica. They breed in huge colonies on the Antarctic Peninsula and build their nests just out of pecking range of one another.

IN FOCUS

BREEDING Emperor penguins trek inland to breed. The males incubate the eggs on their feet for two months during the bitter winter, while females go to sea to feed. When the females return, they bring food for the newly hatched chicks.

Penguins leaping onto land

Spyhopping

Orcas regularly "spyhop"—hold their heads above water for periods of time. Experts think they are watching for prey.

Food for many

Shrimplike krill are only 2 inches (5 cm) long, but they are one of the most important food items in the ocean. Birds, fish, and even whales feed on these tiny creatures.

Fierce hunters

Leopard seals are the most ferocious of all seals and have sharp-toothed jaws for attacking prey. Penguins are their main food, and they lie in wait to catch the birds as they dive into the water.

Ice fish

Antarctic waters are too cold for some fish, but the Antarctic ice fish has its own "antifreeze" in its body. This keeps it from freezing.

Lützow-Holm Bay
Cape Ann
Enderby Land
Cape Boothby
MacDonald Islands
Heard Island
Cooperation Sea
Prince Charles Mtns
Cape Darnley
Amery Ice Shelf
Prydz Bay
West Ice Shelf
Cape Penck
Shackleton Ice Shelf
East
Antarctica
Vincennes Bay
Davis Sea
Cape Poinsett
Wilkes Land
Cape Goodenough
Porpoise Bay
Mawson Sea
Cape Morse
Adélie Land
South Magnetic Pole
Fisher Bay
Dumont d'Urville Sea
S

Indian Ocean

Yellow-lipped sea krait

THE THIRD LARGEST of the world's oceans, the Indian Ocean lies between Africa, Asia, and Australia. It covers an area more than five times the size of the United States, and its deepest point is the Java Trench, which plunges 23,376 feet (7,125 m) deep. Unlike the Atlantic and Pacific, the Indian Ocean does not extend into the far north—its northernmost part is the Persian Gulf—and it is the warmest of all the oceans. Its waters contain many coral reefs, and it is also home to a wide range of sharks.

Red-billed tropic bird

Beautiful, graceful tropic birds spend most of their lives soaring over the sea. They dive down and plunge into the water to seize fish and squid.

Coral communities

The Red Sea is part of the Indian Ocean, and there are some particularly rich coral reefs in its clear waters.

Olive ridley turtle

The ridley is only about 2 feet (60 cm) long and is one of the smallest sea turtles. It lives in warm waters and preys on jellyfish, snails, and shrimp.

Cephalic lobes help funnel food into the manta's mouth

Lionfish

Sharp fins are linked to venom glands

This extraordinary fish lurks among coral reefs and catches other fish and shrimp with its speedy movements. It uses its venomous fins to defend itself from predators.

Sperm whale

This whale's huge head contains up to 500 gallons (1,900 L) of waxy oil. This may help the whale adjust its buoyancy as it dives, but no one really knows. The whale can grow up to 59 feet (18 m) long.

Nautilus

Inside the nautilus's shell is a soft-bodied creature with lots of tentacles. It is related to the octopus and squid.

Giant fish

The whale shark is the largest of all fish and can grow to 45 feet (13.5 m) long. This giant feeds mostly on shrimplike krill, but it does also eat other fish.

IN FOCUS

ANCIENT FISH Coelacanths were thought to have become extinct at the time of the dinosaurs. But the fish were rediscovered in 1938, living in the deep sea of the Indian Ocean.

Coelacanth fossils show that this fish has remained unchanged. Its paired fins move in the same way as our legs.

Manta ray

Manta rays grow up to 23 feet (7 m) wide and are the largest rays. These fish regularly migrate 700 miles (1,100 km) across the Indian Ocean.

Atlantic Ocean

Caribbean spiny lobster

THE SECOND LARGEST of the world's oceans, the Atlantic covers about one-fifth of Earth's surface, about 28.7 million square miles (74.3 million km²). This includes a number of shallow seas, such as the Caribbean, Mediterranean, and North seas. A huge underwater mountain range called the Mid-Atlantic Ridge extends from Iceland to south of South Africa, and some of its highest peaks rise above the surface, forming islands. The Atlantic contains some of the world's richest fishing areas.

Birth of an ocean

The Atlantic was formed 150 million years ago, when Europe and North America broke apart and Africa and South America also separated.

Puffin

The puffin is a good swimmer and uses its wings to propel itself along underwater. It hunts small fish, such as sandeels, which it gathers in its large, colorful beak.

▶▶ **FIT FOR LIFE**

FLYING FISH This fish actually leaps above the water's surface to escape its enemies. Once out of the water, it can glide as far as 655 feet (200 m).

Ocean surface

Winglike fins help lift the fish out of the water

Northern gannet

These seabirds gather in huge colonies of many thousands on rocks and small islands in the Atlantic to mate. Each pair lays a single egg in a nest made on the ground.

IN FOCUS

DEEP-SEA DWELLERS Below about 3,300 feet (1,000 m), the sea is completely dark and there are few living creatures. Those fish that do manage to survive down here have evolved ways of tackling any prey they can find.

Black swallower A huge stomach allows this fish to eat prey larger than itself.

Gelatinous blindfish This little fish lives on the seabed, snapping up any scraps that come its way.

Deep-sea angler fish The angler has its own fishing rod—a lure that glows in the darkness to attract prey.

Gulper eel This fish's huge mouth opens very wide so it can swallow large prey.

Atlantic mackerel

These fast-swimming fish gather in groups called schools, which move together in surface waters. They feed on smaller fish, such as sandeels.

Atlantic bluefin tuna

The sleek, streamlined body of this fish helps it cut through the water at high speed, up to 43 miles per hour (70 km/h). It migrates between feeding and breeding sites and crosses the Atlantic several times a year.

Hagfish

This primitive fish has no scales and no jaws, only a slitlike mouth surrounded by tentacles. It bores into dead fish with its rasping tongue.

Marlin leaping out of the sea

Blue marlin

The blue marlin is one of the largest of all fish and can measure 14 feet (4.3 m) long. It moves very fast and uses its spearlike upper jaw to attack schools of smaller fish.

Pacific Ocean

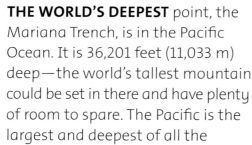

Hawaiian turkeyfish

THE WORLD'S DEEPEST point, the Mariana Trench, is in the Pacific Ocean. It is 36,201 feet (11,033 m) deep—the world's tallest mountain could be set in there and have plenty of room to spare. The Pacific is the largest and deepest of all the oceans, and it covers about one-third of the world's surface. Its average depth is about 14,000 feet (4,000 m), and its widest point is between Indonesia and the coast of Colombia, which is a distance of about 12,300 miles (19,800 km).

Kelp forest

Kelp is a kind of giant seaweed that grows to 160 feet (50 m) long. Huge kelp forests in the northeast Pacific provide food and shelter for many kinds of fish and other animals.

IN DANGER! The leatherback is the largest of all sea turtles and grows up to 7 feet (2 m) long. It is now critically endangered, mostly because so many of its eggs are stolen from nests, and animals are accidentally caught in fishing nets.

Sooty shearwater

These common seabirds dive for food such as fish and shellfish. They nest on islands. Each pair digs a long burrow where they care for their single egg.

IN FOCUS

BIGGEST ANIMAL The blue whale is the largest animal that has ever lived. It measures up to 100 feet (30 m) long. Despite its great size, the whale feeds on tiny shrimplike creatures called krill, and it may eat 40 million of these a day.

Tail fluke

Fast swimmer The whale's streamlined shape helps it move at 23 miles per hour (37 km/h).

Diving seabird
The brown booby makes spectacular dives into the water from up to 50 feet (15 m) above the surface to capture prey.

Wings held back to streamline the body

A humpback leaps above the water's surface

Schooling fish such as anchovies are a favorite prey

Singing whales
Humpback whales keep in touch with one another by their complex songs. Males also sing to attract females and may serenade for hours on end. No one knows why these whales leap from the water—perhaps it's just for fun!

Dall's porpoise
The largest porpoise, this sea mammal lives only in the northern Pacific where it feeds on fish and squid.

The shark has one eye at each end of its head

Hammerhead shark
The underside of this shark's strange-shaped head is lined with electrical detectors. These pick up the tiny electrical signals given off by other animals and help the shark track down its prey.

Giant clam
This is one of the world's biggest mollusks, and it lives 100 years or more. It grows up to 4 feet (1.2 m) long and weighs more than 440 pounds (200 kg).

Glossary

amphibian A vertebrate animal that can live on land and in water. Salamanders, frogs, and toads are all amphibians.

antlers Bony structures on the head of an animal such as a deer.

ape A large, tail-less mammal, related to monkeys. Apes include gorillas, chimpanzees, and gibbons.

carcass The body of a dead animal.

carnivorous A carnivorous animal is one that feeds on the flesh of other animals. Strictly speaking, a carnivore is a member of the mammal group Carnivora, which includes lions, wolves, and smaller creatures such as weasels.

carrion The bodies of animals that have died naturally or been killed by other animals.

colony A number of individuals of a single species that live together in one place. Termites, ants, and many kinds of bees and wasps live in colonies.

conservation The efforts made to protect animals and the natural world for the future.

coral Small animals that live in large groups, or colonies, in the sea. A coral reef is made up of the hard skeletons of coral animals.

Charles Darwin An English naturalist who lived in the 19th century. He is best known for his theories on the evolution of life.

deciduous A deciduous tree is one that loses all its leaves in the fall and grows new leaves in the spring.

delta The low land at the mouth of a river where it flows into the sea. At some deltas, the river branches into many channels as it nears the sea.

dominant A dominant animal is the leader of a pack or group.

echolocation Used by bats and whales to help them find prey. The animal makes a high-pitched sound and then uses the echoes that bounce off any object in its path to work out where and how big that object is.

ecosystem The whole environment of an area, in which animals and plants interact with each other. A tropical rainforest is an ecosystem and so is a coral reef.

endangered Describes a rare creature that is in danger of becoming extinct.

Equator An imaginary line around the center of Earth at an equal distance from the North and South Poles.

evolution The process of change and adaptation in living things over time.

extinct Describes a species of animal that is no longer in existence.

fungi (fungus) Fungi are simple living things that are neither plants nor animals. Examples of fungi are mushrooms and molds.

gland A part of the body that produces special substances such as poisons. A skunk makes the smelly liquid it uses to defend itself in scent glands.

habitat The surroundings in which an animal lives.

hibernation When an animal hibernates, it goes into a deep sleep. A hibernating animal's body temperature and heart rate drop to save energy during the winter, when food is often scarce.

invertebrate An animal without a backbone. Insects, spiders, and animals such as crabs, worms, and snails are all invertebrates.

larva A young form of an animal, which looks different from the adult. A caterpillar is the larva of a butterfly.

mammal A warm-blooded animal, usually with four legs and a covering of hair or fur, that gives birth to fully formed young. Female mammals feed their young on milk from their mammary glands.

mangrove A mangrove tree is a kind of plant, usually with aerial roots, that grows on swampy tropical coasts and can survive in salt water. An area where lots of mangroves grow is called a mangrove forest.

marsupial A kind of mammal that gives birth to very small, immature young, which are then carried in a pouch on the female's body while they grow.

migration The movement of groups of animals from one region to another in order to find the best conditions for feeding or breeding. A migratory animal is one that makes migrations.

mollusk A type of invertebrate such as a snail, slug, or clam, many of which have a hard shell. Squid and octopus are also mollusks.

nectar A sweet liquid inside flowers. Many birds and insects feed on nectar.

parasite An animal that lives on or inside the body of another animal and depends on it for food.

pesticide Something that is used to destroy or drive away weeds or creatures such as some insects and other animals that damage crops.

plankton Tiny plants and animals that live in water. Most can only be seen through a microscope.

pollution The introduction of things that damage the natural world, such as garbage and oil.

polyp A small barrel-shaped animal, such as a sea anemone or coral, with a mouth surrounded by tentacles at the top end.

prairie A type of grassland, typically found in North America.

predator A creature that hunts and kills other creatures to eat.

prehensile A part of an animal's body, such as a tail, that can grasp things. Some snakes have a prehensile tail, which they use like an extra limb to hold on to branches.

prey Animals that are hunted and eaten by other animals.

primate The group of mammals to which monkeys, apes, and humans belong. Most primates have a large brain and grasping hands.

quill A sharp spine on a porcupine. Birds' feathers are also sometimes called quills.

rainforest Forests near the Equator, which are hot and wet all year round.

reptile A vertebrate animal with scaly skin. Tortoises, snakes, lizards, and crocodiles are all reptiles. Most reptiles lay eggs with tough, leathery shells.

rodent A member of the mammal group Rodentia, which includes rats, mice, and squirrels.

saliva The liquid in an animal's mouth—also called spit.

savanna An area of grassland, usually in a tropical region. The largest savannas are in Africa.

scavenger An animal that feeds on the remains of creatures that have died naturally or been killed by other flesh eaters.

school A group of fish that swims together.

scythe A hand tool used to cut grass or other crops.

species A type of plant or animal. Members of the same species can mate and produce young that can themselves bear young.

talon The sharp claw of an animal such as an eagle.

tentacle The long body parts of an animal such as a squid.

tropical Describes the hot regions of the world around the Equator.

tundra A very cold, treeless area with low-growing plants in the far north or high on mountains.

venom A liquid made by snakes or other animals that is used to kill or paralyze their prey.

vertebrate An animal with a backbone. Mammals, birds, reptiles, amphibians, and fish are all vertebrates.

wattle A fleshy flap on the head or neck of some birds.

Index

ATLAS OF ANIMALS

ATLAS OF ANIMALS

Credits and Acknowledgments

Key: c = center; r = right; l = left; b = bottom; t = top; cr = center right; cl = center left; br = bottom right; bl = bottom left; bc = bottom center; tc = top center; bcr = bottom center right; bcl = bottom center left; tcr = top center right; tcl = top center left; bg = background

Cover

Front cover tl iS, tc CBT, tr TPL, cl TPL and illustrations by Peter Bull Art Studio
Back cover illustration by Jon Gittoes

Photographs

ALA = Alamy; **AUS** = Auscape International; **CBT** = Corbis; **DSC** = Digital Stock; **iS** = iStockphoto.com; **MP** = Minden Picture; **NGS** = National Geographic Society; **NHPA** = Photoshot; **NPL** = Nature Picture Library; **SH** = Shutterstock; **SP** = SeaPics; **SPL** = Science Photo Library; **TPL** = photolibrary.com; **Wiki** = Wikipedia

1c iS; 2tc iS; bl, br SH; 2-3bg iS; 4bc, c, tr iS; cl MP; cr TPL; 5c AUS; br, cl, cr, tl iS; tr SH; 6bc, c, cl iS; 7bc, br, cr iS; 8cl NPL; bl SPL; 8-9tc CBT; 9c ALA; cl, cr iS; br SH; 10bl, cl NHPA; 11cl iS; tr NHPA; 12bl, tc iS; bc MP; c NHPA; 13bl, c, cr iS; br NHPA; tc TPL; 14bl, br, tc iS; cl NHPA; c TPL; 14-15c, tc TPL; 15bc NHPA; c, cl, cr, tr TPL; 18tl iS; 19bc, bl, c, cr iS; br MP; 20cr iS; br, cl MP; 20-21bc iS; 21cr CBT; tc iS; cr SH; 22cl iS; c NHPA; br TPL; 23bl, br iS; tc MP; bc, cl TPL; 24cl NHPA; cr TPL; 25c CBT; cl, tl iS; br, c, cr MP; 26c SH; 27bc, cr iS; tl MP; 28cl iS; c MP; bl TPL; 29tl MP; c, cr TPL; 30tl iS; c SH; cr TPL; 31tr iS; br MP; bl, cr TPL; 32tc, tr SH; 33bc, bl, br iS; tr MP; br, cr TPL; 34bc, bl, c, tl iS; cl TPL; 35cl MP; bc NHPA; 36c, cl, cr iS; 37c iS; tl MP; 38c, cl, cr iS; br MP; tl NHPA; 38-39tc MP; 39c, tl MP; br SH; 40bc iS; tl NHPA; c, cl TPL; 41c, tr iS; bl, br, tl TPL; 42bl, tl NHPA; cl, cr TPL; 42-43bc TPL; 43cl, iS; c MP; br SH; cr TPL; 44c CBT; br, cl iS; bl, tl NHPA; cr TPL; 45br, tl iS; tr NHPA; 46tc SH; 47bc, br, cr iS; br NHPA; bc SH; c TPL; 48bl, tl iS; cl, cr SH; 49br iS; bc, cl SH; 50cr CBT; tl NPL; bc, bl SH; cl TPL; 50-51bc SH; 51bc, cr iS; br, tl, tr SH; 52cl, tl NHPA; 53br, tcr, tl, tr NHPA; bcr NPL; 54c, cl iS; tl NPL; bl, br SH; 55bc, bl, tr NHPA; cr NPL; tc SH; 56br, c iS; cl NHPA; bl SH; 57tl NHPA; cl SH; 58bc iS; cl NPL; cr Wiki; 58-59bc TPL; 59cl iS; bc NHPA; tr SH; br, tc TPL; cr Wiki; 60bcl, tr iS; c NHPA; bc, bl, cl SH; c, tcl TPL; 61br iS; 62bl, br, cr iS; cl TPL; 63bc iS; cr NHPA; 64cl CBT; bl, br, c iS; c NHPA; tl SH; 65tc iS; tl NHPA; c SH; cr TPL; 66c iS; cl MP; 66-67b MP; 67c NHPA; 68cl NHPA; 69tr CBT; bcr, c, tl iS; tcr SH; 70cl CBT; c iS; bl NHPA; 71tr CBT; bc, br, tl iS; cl MP; c TPL; 72cl iS; c NHPA; tl TPL; 72-73c NHPA; 73br, tc iS; bc, bl, tr NHPA; cr TPL; 74cl NHPA; bcr, tl TPL; 75tr iS; c MP; cl NHPA; bc, br, c TPL; 76bl, cl iS; bc, tc SH; 77br, c, cr, tc, tr iS; c, cr SH; 78bl iS; cl MP; c NHPA; tl NPL; 78-79bc SH; 79c iS; bl MP; cr NHPA; tr NPL; tl SH; 80c iS; cl, tl NHPA; bl NPL; 80-81bc iS; 81bc, tc MP; br, tl, tr NHPA; bcl NPL; cr TPL; 82br iS; cl MP; bl NHPA; c, tl NPL; 83tcr CBT; tr iS; bcr, bl, br NHPA; cl, tc NPL; 84cl NPL; tl Wiki; 85bc iS; bl, br, tl, tr NHPA; cl NPL; cr TPL; 86cl MP; bc SH; 87cr, tc iS; bc, tc, tl NHPA; bl NPL; 88bl iS; bc, cl NHPA; cr TPL; 89tr NHPA; c, tc, tl TPL; 90bl iS; c, cl NPL; 90-91bc NPL; 91tl CBT; br NHPA; tc, tr NPL; c TPL; 92cr CBT; tc iS; br, c NHPA; tl TPL; 93br iS; bl NHPA; c, tc SH; 94br iS; 95br, cr, tc, tr iS; tr NHPA; 96cl iS; br, c MP; bl NHPA; tl Wiki; 97tr AUS; tc, tl NHPA; 98bc, bl, cr iS; cl NHPA; bc TPL; 99tl NHPA; c TPL; 100bl NHPA; cl TPL; 101cr tl AUS; tr NHPA; 102c, cl iS; cr NHPA; 103tc iS; bl, br NHPA; 104cl iS; c MP; 105cr iS; cl, tc, tr TPL; 106bc, bl, br, cl, cr TPL; 107tl CBT; bl, br, c, cl, tl NHPA; 108tcl AUS; bc DSC; c NGS; bcl, cr NPL; 108-109br AUS; c DSC; 110bc iS; bc, bl MP; br, cl TPL; 111tr NPL; 112cl, tl; 113c iS; cr NHPA; bl SH; 114bl, cl, cr iS; 115c MP; cr SP; bl, tr TPL; 116c iS; cl MP; bl NPL; 117cl, tr iS; br NHPA; cr, tl TPL; 118br, c, cl iS; 119tl iS; bc, bl, cr TPL; 120bc, br NHPA; cl, cr SP; 121cr iS; tr MP; br TPL.

Illustrations

ABar = Alistair Barnard; **ABoo** = Andre Boos; **ABow** = Anne Bowman; **BCal** = Bob & Clara Calhoun/Bruce Coleman Limited; **BCro** = Barry Croucher/The Art Agency; **BE** = Brin Edwards/The Art Agency; **CE** = Christer Eriksson; **CJ** = Contact Jupiter/Yvan Meunier; **CL** = Connell Lee; **CS** = Chris Shields; **CT** = Claude Thivierge; **DC** = Dan Cole/The Art Agency; **DK** = David Kirshner; **ER** = Edwina Riddle; **FD** = Fiammetta Dogi; **FK** = Frank Knight; **FW** = Frank Wright; **GT** = Guy Trougton; **GW** = Genevieve Wallace; **IJ** = Ian Jackson/The Art Agency; **IM** = Iain McKellar; **JB** = Jane Beatson; **JD** = Jane Dunstan/The Art Agency; **JF** = John Francis/Bernard Thornton Artists, UK; **JG** = Jon Gittoes; **JMac** = John Mac/Folio; **JMcK** = James McKinnon; **KS** = Kevin Stead; **LC** = Leonello Calvetti; **MA** = Mark Atkinson/Garden Studio; **MC** = Martin Camm; **MDan** = Marc Dando; **MDon** = Mike Donnelly/The Art Agency; **MGoo** = Malcolm Goodwin; **MGro** = Magic Group; **MP** = Mick Posen/The Art Agency; **MT** = Myke Taylor; **PBac** = Paul Bachem;

PBul = Peter Bull Art Studio; **PSch** = Peter Schouten; **PSco** = Peter Scott/The Art Agency; **RB** = Richard Bonson/The Art Agency; **RC** = Robin Carter/The Art Agency; **RG** = Ray Grinaway; **RMan** = Rob Mancini; **RMor** = Robert Morton; **SA** = Susanna Addario; **SD** = Sandra Doyle/The Art Agency; **SH** = Steve Hobbs; **SJC** = Stuart Jackson-Carter/The Art Agency; **SO** = Stan Osolinksi; **TB** = Thomas Bayley/The Art Agency; **TH** = Tim Hayward; **TP** = Tony Pyrzakowski; **TR** = Trevor Ruth; **WA** = Wildlife Art

4tl CT; 6-7c CE; 7tr DK; tr SD; 8tl ABow; tr RB; 9tr GT; 10c MDon; 10-11bc, tc IJ; bc TR; 12tl PSch; 14tl CS; 18br CE; tr DK; c FD; cl FK; br GT; c GW; cr IJ; tl JB; c LC; cr, tc MGro; tc MS; 20tl DK; tr FD; cl SD; 21br DC; tl, tl FD; tr PBul; tc, tr RC; 22bl FW; tl GT; 23tc JMcK; 24tl KS; 24-25b CL; 25bl GW; tr SO; 26bl BCro; c BCal; bc LC; tl SA; cl TR; 26-27b BE; 27br CS; tr JD; bc MGro; 28tl GT; 28-29b BE; 29c, tc, tr IJ; br MGro; 30c CE; 31tc MGro; tl RC; 32bc, tc, tl DK; tl GT; c, tl JB; cl JG; c PBul; cr RMan; 33cl DK; 34tr JD; 34-35bc FK; 35br ABow; 36bc MP; tl PBul; cl WA; 37cr MDon; cl PBul; bl TP; 38b JMac; 38-39b DK; 39tc BE; r, tr GT; br MGro; 40br DC; b DK; 41l CJ; c RM; 43tr DK; tl FK; 44bl IJ; 45bc, bl JD; c MP; 46cl FK; c IJ; bl MDon; br TH; 47tr CS; bcl DK; tc MC; tcr SA; bl, tcl TH; 48c DK; 49tr IJ; tl IM; 52bl, c DC; 52-53bc SJC; 55tl SJC; 56tl MT; 56-57br IJ; 57tc JG; tr KS; 58bl DK; tl TH; 60br, cr DK; 61tr CE; bc, c, cl DK; bcl, tc GT; c RG; 62tl RG; bc RMan; 63tc JD; cl MGro; 62-63b SH; 65tr DC; br PBul; 66tl DK; bl TH; 67br CT; tl PBac; tc, tr SH; 68tl GT; cr MGro; 68-69b CE; 69bc GT; bl MC; 70tl MGro; 70-71bc SJC; 71tc GT; 72bc TR; 74tcr ABar; bc PBul; 75tc, tl DK; tc MGro; 76bcr, c, tcr DK; br MDon; 77bl, tl FK; cl MGro; 79br FK; 83c PBul; 84bl DK; br PBul; 86tl DK; br GT; 86-87c ABoo; 87br DK; 88tl DK; 88-89br SJC; 90tl MGro; 91tc DK; bl FK; 92bc, bl ER; 93cl ER; tr JD; tl PBul; 94cl CE; bl DC; bcr DK; bc GT; c MA; tr PBul; tcr RG; 95bcl, bl, tcl GT; bc PSco; tc RG; c SLC; 96cr DK; 97br CE; bl DC; cl GT; 98-99br DK; 98tl DK; 99tr DC; 100bc DK; tl JF; 100-101bc SD; 101c MA; cl RG; br SLC; 102bl, br GT; tl DK; 102-103c GT; 103cr SD; 104tl DK; 104-105tc GT; b SJC; 106tl DK; 107tr DK; 108tl DK; 109tr BE; tl DK; 110c MP; tl RMor; 112bl, c CJ; br TP; 113br CE; tr CJ; 114tl MP; 115br LC; 116tl DK; 116-117bc RC; 117bc DK; 118bl MGoo; tl TR; 119br DA; c, tl, tr RC; 120bl LC; tl RC; 120-121bc TB; 121c CE; tl DC; 122bl KS; 122-123tc IJ; 123br CE; tc MGro; 124bl CE; tc SD; 125tr CE; 126bc DK; 127tl CE; bc DK; 128br DK.

Maps and Graphs

Original maps by Will Pringle/Map Graphx and Laurie Whiddon/Map Illustrations, adapted by Peter Cooling.

Infographics by Andrew Davies/Creative Communication.